TERRY BOYLE

DISCOVER ONTARIO

STORIES OF THE PROVINCE'S UNIQUE PEOPLE AND PLACES

DUNDURN
TORONTO

Editor: Jennifer McKnight
Design: Jennifer Gallinger
Cover design: Sarah Beaudin
Cover image: Courtesy of the Ontario Archives.
Printer: Webcom

Library and Archives Canada Cataloguing in Publication

Boyle, Terry, author
        Discover Ontario : stories of the province's unique people and places / Terry Boyle.

Includes bibliographic references and index.
Issued in print and electronic formats.
ISBN 978-1-4597-3220-9 (paperback).--ISBN 978-1-4597-3221-6 (pdf).--
ISBN 978-1-4597-3222-3 (epub)

        1. Ontario--History, Local--Anecdotes. 2. Ontario--History, Local--
Guidebooks. I. Title.

FC3061.B685 2016   971.3   C2015-908469-5
                                            C2015-908470-9

1   2   3   4   5   20   19   18   17   16

We acknowledge the support of the Canada Council for the Arts and the Ontario Arts Council for our publishing program. We also acknowledge the financial support of the Government of Canada through the Canada Book Fund and Livres Canada Books, and the Government of Ontario through the Ontario Book Publishing Tax Credit and the Ontario Media Development Corporation.

Care has been taken to trace the ownership of copyright material used in this book. The author and the publisher welcome any information enabling them to rectify any references or credits in subsequent editions.
                                                                — J. Kirk Howard, President

The publisher is not responsible for websites or their content unless they are owned by the publisher.

VISIT US AT
Dundurn.com | @dundurnpress | Facebook.com/dundurnpress | Pinterest.com/dundurnpress

Dundurn
3 Church Street, Suite 500
Toronto, Ontario, Canada
M5E 1M2

In memory of Bob Rowe,
a good friend and mentor

————

Thanks to my wife, Allanah O'Boyle,
for assisting in the editing of this book

CONTENTS

Introduction   11

MEMORIES OF ONTARIO

Fishing   17
Lost North America   20
The Irish: Part 1   22
The Irish: Part 2   25
The Need to Remember   27
From the Sixties and Beyond   30
Prohibition   32
The Great Depression   36
Elders' Conference, 1992   40
Nature in Victoria County   42
Memories of Ontario   45
The Brougham Apple Basket   48
Bancroft Rock Festival   50
Demographics   52
Shipwreck   55
A Young Bride's Dream   59

THE PARANORMAL AND THE UNEXPLAINED

The Mysteries of Long Point   65
Strange Creatures Swimming in Our Waters   68
Strange Lights in the Sky   71
The Discovery of the Crystal Skull   74
The Agawa Pictographs of Lake Superior   77
Beyond the Grave   79
Saving Lives on the French River   82
The Roswell Crash   85
Project Magnet   91
The Aboriginal Haunting in Orillia   95
Fairies and the Elemental World   98
A Pioneer of Paranormal Research   102
The Ghost Road   105
Alien Encounter in Ontario   108
The Mound Builders   111
Serpent Mounds   113
Ghosts   115
Who Murdered Billy Stone?   120

INTERESTING RESIDENTS

Sheriff Nelson Reynolds   125
Joseph Bigelow   128
George Reid, the Painter   131
Franklin and the Northwest Passage   133
David Boyle   136
David Suzuki   139
Gerald Sinclair Hayward   141
Grey Owl   144

LOCAL INTEREST

Oil Springs: The Oil Capital of North America   149
Collingwood   154

Sarnia   157
London   159
Southampton   162
Penryn, Port Hope   165
The Dream of Owning a Castle   167
Ravensworth, Cobourg   169
The Mackenzie Estate, Kirkfield   172
Perth   175
Cornwall   177
Brooklin   179
Scugog Island   181
Stirling   183
Niagara Falls   186
Penmarvian, Paris   189
Wasaga Beach   191
Kincardine   194
Elora   197
The Conant Homestead, Oshawa   200
Moose Factory and Moosonee   202
Gores Landing   206
Long Beach   209
Oakville   212
Sudbury   215
Sault Ste. Marie   217
Gravenhurst and Bracebridge   219
Cochrane   223
Rodman Hall, St. Catharines   226

Bibliography   229
Index   233

INTRODUCTION

My career in radio began by chance in 1987, when a radio salesman by the name of Bob Rowe arrived at my place of business. Bob and I exchanged some words and quickly realized that we had quite a lot in common. As a journalist I had written several books, and Bob had spent a career in public relations. In other words our meeting was a synchronicity, to say the least.

Bob commented on my voice and asked me if I had ever worked in radio. I said no, but I had studied broadcast journalism at one time. He then asked me if I might consider working in radio as a broadcaster. I hadn't really thought about it, but I asked him what he had in mind. He stated that the station he worked for, Classical 96.3 and 103.1 FM, had a spot to fill after the Saturday noon-hour news. A brief commentary, three minutes in length, would do the trick. He added that I could highlight people, places, and events going on in Ontario. In fact, they could call the show "Discover Ontario with Terry Boyle." Bob felt that a show of that nature would prove to be an asset to the station.

"Wow," was my only reply.

Bob asked me to write some copy and come down to the station and record a demo tape. In those days the radio station was located in a small plaza in Cobourg, Ontario. After some consideration, I proceeded to write a show and tape a demo. It was a hit and I was suddenly on air.

This book, *Discover Ontario*, is a collection of radio shows spanning 1987 to 1997. I have attempted to select informative, interesting, and thought-provoking shows for your reading pleasure. Some stories have been brought up to date with a note at the end.

The book includes stories like that of Project Magnet, which was a Canadian government top-secret mission during the 1950s involving the study and observation of unidentified flying objects.

Buried treasure always seems to appeal to the metal-detector enthusiasts, and the mystery of Long Point should attract some interest. A chest of gold was buried there by trader David Ramsey, shortly after he killed three Aboriginal people during a drunken binge.

Then there is Dr. Troyer, who was convinced that he was being kidnapped at night by witches. In order to procure some safety from these creatures he designed and built a witch trap. This apparatus is now on display in the museum in the town of Simcoe.

Creature features are always a hit. Here you'll find a show about a water snake measuring thirty feet in length and fifteen inches in diameter sighted in Lake Ontario off the shore of St. Catharines. Or, how about the seven-foot alligator that attacked a young girl at Fraser Lake near Bancroft in September of 1925?

Discover more about the Mitchell-Hedges Crystal Skull (a feature in the last Indiana Jones film) that was found in the ancient City Of Fallen Stones. What is this ancient relic's connection to Ontario?

There are stories of the paranormal, flying saucers, and alien visits. Read about the attempted murder that took place at Ravensworth in Cobourg or the fatal Whitby shooting of a telegraph operator.

Enjoy historical profiles of communities such as Collingwood, Sarnia, Southampton, Cornwall, Brooklin, Scugog Island, and Kincardine, to name a few.

Whatever your cup of tea, Discover Ontario will delight and entertain you. I hope you enjoy reading the book as much as I loved writing and narrating the stories on radio.

I have increased the length of some radio shows from their original format to give you a more complete understanding of the subject matter than could be done in my three-minute limitations on air.

Since my decision to take a break from radio, Classical 96.3 and 103.1 FM has grown into a much larger radio station with expanded listenership and geographical presence. The old studio in Cobourg is long gone, along with some of the wonderful people I met and with whom I worked. The station is now located on Queen Street in downtown Toronto.

As for my good friend Bob Rowe, he has passed on to the other side. I have dedicated this book to him in honour of our time together and for his remarkable kindness and friendship.

Enjoy.

Terry Boyle
Burk's Falls, Ontario

MEMORIES OF ONTARIO

FISHING

At some time in the first quarter of the nineteenth century someone developed commercial fishing on Georgian Bay. The introduction of fishing to the Thirty Thousand Islands region was achieved through the natural extension of operations further down the Great Lakes.

Georgian Bay fishery grew in time to be the greatest source of lake trout and whitefish on all the Canadian lakes. The east side of the bay, with its deep water and sandy shoals, suited these fish well.

In the 1850s, Georgian Bay harvest was upwards of a thousand barrels annually. When the railroad reached the south end of Georgian Bay, circa 1860, a more direct route to market was opened, and Collingwood, Meaford, and Owen Sound became the major fishing ports of Georgian Bay.

The expansion of the fishing market prompted more vessels to sail out each spring to the various fishing grounds in the bay. The men who fished some distance from home built a fishing station on the outer fringes of the Thirty Thousand Islands. The largest station was at the Bustard Islands. There were others at the Minks, the Snakes, and Champlain Island. These were sizeable summer colonies, made up of a number of fishermen and their families.

Improved transportation made it possible to market fish in very fresh condition. United States buyers sent schooners on regular rounds to collect the fish at the stations, packing them in ice in great wheeled boxes with a capacity of half a ton, that could be rolled on and off the

Courtesy of the Ontario Archives.

The largest fishing station on Georgian Bay was situated at the Bustard Islands. By the 1850s, the Georgian Bay fish harvest was over one thousand barrels annually.

schooners. One of the best available descriptions we have of the fishing industry in the nineteenth century is contained in the book entitled *The Georgian Bay*, written by C.L. Hamilton in 1893. After a sailing excursion on the bay he stated, "There were then over 400 men engaged in fishing in Georgian Bay, and equipment included 150 boats, 15 tugs and one and a half million yards of nets. An outfit for two men, a boat and sails, and three gangs of nets was valued at around $1100. In a season, these men would take perhaps twenty tons of fish, for which the buyer's agent would pay seventy dollars to eighty dollars a ton." Mr. Hamilton also recorded that there was a small trade in fish oil at the time.

In the 1930s the sea lamprey entered Lake Huron and destroyed the lake trout population there. At first the Georgian Bay fish seemed to resist the invader from the Atlantic, but by 1960 there were no trout left in the fishing grounds. Other fish were attacked by the lamprey, the most important of them the whitefish. In 1959, the total catch amounted to only 14,515 kilograms of fish.

Large-scale commercial fishing in Georgian Bay came to a close. Today there are still a few commercial fishermen working their nets. However, when a licensed fishermen retires the government buys back his or her licence and usually does not reissue it. Therefore, the commercial fishermen are becoming a dying breed, just like the fish themselves. More questions need to be asked of our politicians regarding the restocking and current levels of fish in the Great Lakes. Restaurants operating in our tourist destinations in Georgian Bay never know if the commercial fishermen will be able to fill their orders or what will happen when the last commercial fisherman disappears. Their businesses may very well vanish like the fishermen and the fish before them.

Courtesy of the Ontario Archives

A young boy stands proudly by the catch of the day.

LOST NORTH AMERICA

When I recently went on a tour of the New England states in search of lost America, I realized the story told about North American heritage in schools and other official places may be entirely fabricated. Do we really believe that Christopher Columbus was the first to discover America? If not, then why do we continue to tell the story?

Remember, our story is of our own creation. The tales we believe about ancestors become the basis for understanding ourselves and our land. This influences our actions in the present. Any fabrication about our origins keeps us in the dark about our truth and about the original people of North America.

The genocide that followed in the wake of Christopher Columbus in North America, and Cortes in Mexico, resulted in the death of approximately eighty million indigenous people beginning in the sixteenth century. Political power, economic expansion, and the consumption of natural resources is merely a continuation of the same destructive forces.

The violence and imbalance will continue until we correct the initial fabrication. That is why the struggle for recognition of truth is so important. Just when we seem to be helpless in the face of huge forces bent on destruction, a creative idea has emerged that has the power to dance us beyond these forces of devastation.

A recent exciting discovery of a great, and complete, stone, solar, and lunar calendar has been made in North Salem, New Hampshire.

Throughout North America, hundreds of stone sites exist. Viking houses have been discovered in Canada that date back to the eleventh and twelfth centuries. Viking artifacts may very well have been found nearly one hundred years ago in Northern Ontario. Iron utensils and weapons of European origin have been unearthed in Canada and in Massachusetts. All over Virginia, Roman nails and iron utensils have presumably been found in undisturbed sites.

A book entitled *Long Before Columbus* highlights a site called Stonehenge in New Hampshire. This ancient site dates back 3,500 years and compares, in many ways, to Stonehenge in England. It is thought to be, and very well could be, of Celtic origin.

Could many of the Aboriginal teachings in North America be a blend of Celtic traditions? Archeological evidence of this sacred site indicates that it was occupied by several distinct groups at various times. Evidence indicates that many sacred sites were not first inhabited by those who are labelled the indigenous peoples of North America.

Archeologists in the past, according to *Long Before Columbus*, have not delved deeply enough to unearth the oldest evidence of ancient peoples in Canada and the United States and their habitation.

The idea that ancient peoples from all over the globe may have graced North America with their presence is exciting. The indigenous people of the Americas may be our own ancestors, considering all the ancient travelling back and forth across the seas. It is truly exciting to imagine what may yet be discovered on this continent.

What revelations are yet to come? Perhaps we can change our story after all and truly alter our current reality to reflect a more global, spiritual matrix on the planet. We are devouring this planet we call home for the sake of economic growth, dominance, and keeping a false ideology alive. It is not North America that is lost but rather our own true heritage.

THE IRISH: PART 1

On the eve of St. Patrick's Day, 1826, Peter Robinson sat in his log mansion in Peterborough to complete his long-overdue accounting of the Irish he had brought to Canada.

Two years had passed since the first contingent had come to the Ottawa Valley. Some people called Robinson too visionary, others questioned why he was dumping paupers on the colony instead of bringing self-sufficient farmers.

Of the 182 families brought to the Ottawa Valley in 1823, a third seemed to have melted away. Robinson could readily account for some who had gone to Perth, Cobourg, and Kingston to ply their trades as carpenters, shoemakers, and bakers. Nine men had gone to the United States as labourers or millwrights. Eight others had died, four by drowning.

People raised to be farmers remained on their granted land. Those who had prospered in the old country tended to prosper in their new habitat. It was challenging to determine the success of these immigrants. Many Irish concealed any good fortune as the slightest sign of wealth in Ireland had meant higher rents and taxes. Some Irish had acquired the habit of begging during the hard years in Ireland, and they begged in Canada even when it was no longer necessary.

One Irish settler, who begged around Perth, was so affluent he was doing it to get money to buy more cattle, happy to wear castoffs and look poverty-stricken.

In the spring of 1826, fifty-eight of Robinson's families were known to be working the land in the area townships. Half a dozen families prospered exceptionally well in Ramsay Township. John Teskey, a Protestant descendant of Rhinelanders who immigrated to County Limerick in the eighteenth century to escape religious conflict, homesteaded on the Mississippi River between Shipman's Mills and Murphy's Falls, where he harnessed the rapids for milling. The hamlet of Appleton was the site of an Indian encampment when the Teskeys arrived, and the Aboriginal peoples came to the mill in their blanket coats, red leggings, and moccasins, curious and silent, to trade venison or a haunch of young bear for flour and pork.

At Clayton Lake, ten miles west of Shipman's Mills, Martin Ryan, from Sixmilebridge in County Clare, had cleared twenty-five acres of thick woodland and acquired ten cows and twelve hogs.

In Ramsay Township the soil was good, but other Irish settlers found themselves on poor or rocky land. John O'Mara considered his land as good as any in the country when he arrived in 1823. He cleared twelve acres before he was finally disillusioned. As acre after acre was laid bare, he saw that his land was poor and rocky.

Hard-working Irishmen clearing rock for a railway line.

Patrick Lynch, from Killarney, cleared twelve acres and found only a crop of barren rock. He suffered further misfortune when his dog and two of his cows were killed by wolves, which he escaped by climbing a tree.

Donald Mackay, in his book *Flight From Famine*, described what the construction of the Rideau Canal meant to the Irish settlers. "When work started on the Rideau Canal in 1826, it provided employment for thousands of Irish for the next six years. The 135 mile canal route travelled from the new village of Bytown on the Ottawa River, along the Rideau Valley toward Kingston through the bush, rock and swamp of eastern Ontario and passed south of the region where Robinson's people had settled."

Those Irish are Canadians now and their dedication to the land and to the earth, itself, is evident wherever they settled. Peter Robinson would be proud today to acknowledge his part in it all.

THE IRISH: PART 2

In 1826 work began on the Rideau Canal, providing employment for thousands of Irish immigrants for the next six years. Many Irish veterans of the Erie and Welland Canals to the southwest, as well as labourers fresh from Ireland, signed up for a job.

Canal engineer John MacTaggert was not fond of the Irish. He stated, "If the Irish can get a mud cabin they will never think of building one of wood. At Bytown, now known as Ottawa, the Irish burrow into sand hills. Smoke is seen issuing out of holes."

The death rate on the canal was high. Unfamiliar with blasting powder, some of the Irish workers blew themselves up, or neglected their wounds and gangrene set in. The most serious hazard lay in drinking polluted water, particularly in what MacTaggert called the infernal place between Rideau Lake and Lake Ontario. The workers would come down with an ailment they called swamp fever. Hundreds of labourers and mechanics were laid down with sickness, many of whom never rose again.

Swamp Fever came on with an attack of fever, dreadful vomiting, pains in the back and loins, and a general loss of appetite. After eight or ten days, jaundice was likely to ensue, and then fits of trembling. The workers very bones ached and their teeth chattered, along with sore ribs. Anyone who had it once was most likely to have a touch of it every year. A moist, hot summer would inevitably foster the disease.

The worst outbreak was amid the lakes and swamps of Newcastle district. Weakened by their ordeal at Kingston, ninety-five Irish settlers died in Peterborough in 1825, and out in the townships more than a thousand were ill. The fever abated during the winter cold, but returned in the spring. Thirty-two people died the next summer and 172 had perished by the end of the year.

One settler wrote, "This fever is the most dreaded by new settlers, and to far too many persons, it has proved a great drawback, especially those people who went into the uncleared lands."

Many people recovered thanks to local doctors and to Aboriginal peoples who taught the settlers the medicinal values of certain plants, such as wild peppermint.

Emily Township received the largest group of Irish settlers. More than one third of the settlers had been ill with the swamp fever. So many men came down with the fever that the women went to work in the clearings, from dawn until well after sundown, burning brush, and planting.

Despite the outbreak of fever, the crop failures, and the exposure of harsh winters, the Irish settlers remained anchored to the land. The hardships they faced cannot even be imagined today.

THE NEED TO REMEMBER

To recycle a ton of paper means to spare nineteen mature trees. A third of the world's rainforests are in Brazil, and this year an area the size of West Germany will be cut and burned. Fifty-seven airlines operating out of Toronto's Pearson Airport will generate twenty-six tons of garbage a day. Our planet will lose twenty-four billion tons of topsoil from over tilling. Ontario businesses produce more than 300,000 tons of waste paper per year. Between 1965 and 1980, in New Brunswick alone, 7.2 million litres of gasoline leaked into the ground.

What on Earth is going on? How much do we really need in order to survive? Have we forgotten our humble beginnings? Mrs. David Fleming of Cobourg, in her eighty-second year, in 1842, created a clear image of how it had once been.

Her story takes us back to 1832, when her father bid farewell to his own father, his mother, and his family and left England for Cobourg. She said:

> My father set sail for the land of promise, Canada, in hope of bettering his circumstances, having heard of this remote country.
>
> Cobourg at that time was little else than a cedar swamp. There were only a few houses and little work to be had, no matter how willingly one would have done it. There was scarcely any money in circulation at that

time, and the brass buttons then worn on the moleskin jackets and trousers would pass for money.

Not long after arriving in Canada, my father and mother met for the first time and in due time were united in marriage. Shortly after my father took up a one hundred acre farm three miles northeast of what is now the village of Baltimore. This land was heavily timbered and not a tree cut on it till my father cut enough to get logs to build a small house. Many a night my father chopped down trees by the light of the moon, and would call my mother out to hear the howling of the timber wolves at no great distance. They were numerous and were often seen in packs of twelve or fifteen. Bears were also plentiful. Deer were also numerous and when clearing up the land we would often find deer horns. The wild pigeons were in immense numbers, flying in great flocks so thick they would darken the sunshine around us. But as the years rolled on, and the land was cleared, the wild pigeons began to disappear till they finally became extinct altogether.

We had very little furniture to decorate with. The house was not very large, being twelve by eighteen feet in size, with no partitions. We were all happy and contented in our humble home, never wishing nor longing for other things we knew nothing about.

About 1859, there was quite an exciting time when word was received that the Prince of Wales was coming to Canada, and would visit Cobourg.

Upwards of seventy years have passed since those memorable days of my childhood. The old pioneers have all passed away and very few of their succeeding generation are left. As I draw near memory — but oh, how changed everything is — no longer a hallowed spot — and with a sad aching heart, and a feeling of loneliness, I turn away. Words cannot describe, for in all probability I will not see it again. If this little sketch interests or gives anyone pleasure, then I feel repaid for writing it.

Mrs. Fleming's story is a call to awaken. It was written circa 1910, more than one hundred years ago, and we still need to be reminded to pay attention in 2016. Imagine!

FROM THE SIXTIES AND BEYOND

The candle flame flickered with each breath. Images danced on the walls, many truths and many lies. The music was poetic, the mood was soft, time never seemed to end, and history was happening before one's eyes. Ontario was alive and the sixties had arrived.

It was a time when thoughts expressed a need for growth of awareness. A new generation had washed up on shore. People were catching their own reflection down by the river, just when Leonard Cohen came along with "Suzanne."

The 1960s was a period of time when young people wanted change, away from the establishment. People looked for a better future. Equality became a buzzword and fashions changed on the scene. People spoke of peace and freedom. They lived in communal settings. Long hair replaced the brush cut. "Give peace a chance" became a slogan. War was wrong. "All You Need Is Love" was a theme song. Everything seemed so cool. Blue jeans replaced corduroys. Running shoes replaced the penny loafer. Rock concerts attracted thousands of people eager to hear the lyrics and rock to the sound. Woodstock was a marker.

During this time I was living in Ontario and attending a number of rock concerts in Toronto. This was the closest thing to Woodstock for my generation. We would often hitchhike from Burlington to Toronto for an event, as we were all too young to own cars in the sixties.

The problem encountered during this period was a lack of clear leadership. Few could envision the potential of this new direction, nor could they see where anyone was really going. When the seventies arrived, people continued with the movement, but although they knew what they did not want, there was no agreement about how to replace it. People went in many directions. The mood changed and the idyllic colours faded. It was still a materialistic world and the struggle for many was too great.

Old rebels became the new establishment. The need to survive financially, to raise families, and to build futures pushed away the world of peace and freedom, but the taste of freedom remained.

Not all individuals abandoned their experiences of the sixties and seventies. Many of the artists, musicians, and writers continued the dream of self-expression and of peace. They continued to work for social change and struggle to end famine and war on the planet. Through the creative process, they continued to trust in a new dawn of awakening expressed in their work. They refused to compromise their ideals.

They found each other and the dawn of a new age was upon them, a new stream of self-consciousness.

Bookstores have shelves of new-age reading material to inspire and to guide the seekers in better ways of living, physically, emotionally, mentally, and spiritually. All was not lost from the generation that rebelled for change in the 1960s. These baby boomers, now approaching their golden years, are still striving for greater purpose, and looking, with enquiry, to the future.

PROHIBITION

The notorious Chicago gangster, Al Capone, symbolized the darker side of American life in the 1920s. He headed an enormous crime syndicate and was thought to have been responsible for more than four hundred gangland killings. He and his mobsters bribed scores of public officials, judges, and law-enforcement agents. Capone ruled Chicago.

Canada had its own version of the American mobster: Rocco Perri of Hamilton. Perri once told a reporter that he was against the use of violence, and yet he headed a brutal gang of criminals in the Niagara Peninsula. Seventeen murders were attributed to the Perri gang, and Perri's wife, Bessie, was shot to death in the garage of their Hamilton home in 1930. Perri disappeared without a trace in 1944 — perhaps a murder victim himself.

Much of the criminal activity in the 1920s and early 1930s resulted from American prohibition. Prohibition was the 18th Amendment to the American Constitution in 1920, and it banned the making, selling, or drinking of liquor in the United States. It was revoked by the 21st Amendment in 1933. By law, the United States was a dry country from 1920–1933, but many "dry" Americans were thirsty and willing to pay good money for illegal alcohol. Profits from bootlegging were enormous. A case of twelve bottles of liquor, bought in Saskatchewan for about fifty dollars, could be sold south of the border for as much as three hundred dollars. Smuggling Canadian liquor into the United States was called rum-running, and it became big business. Some of

Courtesy of the Ontario Archives.

The evils of drink led to naptime in the bush.

Canada's wealthiest families got their start in the trade in illegal alcohol during American prohibition.

Much of the alcohol made and shipped in Canada went to the United States. It is estimated that upwards of 22 million litres of Canadian liquor entered the United States illegally every year during the American prohibition.

Rum-running was common along the largely undefended North American border and down both coasts. The most bootlegging traffic occurred between Windsor, Ontario, and nearby Detroit, Michigan. In warm weather, a fleet of more than eight hundred rum-running speedboats plied the stretch of water between Windsor and Detroit. In winter, dozens of old cars and trucks swarmed across the frozen river with bootleg liquor.

Many Canadians looked on rum-running with amused tolerance. To many, they were modern-day Robin Hoods, cleverly outsmarting, and outrunning American law-enforcement agents. In the United States, bootlegging was a deadly serious, underworld business. The attraction of huge profits from the illegal trade quickly drew machine-gun-toting American mobsters. American mobsters brought with them gang warfare, murder and the wholesale corruption of police, judges and government officials. The lawlessness spilled across the Canadian border and gave some Canadian supporters of prohibition second thoughts. In 1923, a Manitoba supporter lamented that the world had been turned upside down by bootleggers, bandits, and bank robbers.

Canada had tried its own version of prohibition during the First World War. In 1918, every province but Quebec had brought in prohibition laws. Ottawa had taken steps in 1917 and 1918 to place strict limits on the importing, manufacturing, and transporting of liquor. Canadian government officials, however, realized that they were losing money to bootleggers — money that could be a source of government revenue. Moderation leagues, often funded by breweries and distilleries, popped up to argue that the control of liquor was better than an outright ban. Federal prohibition laws lapsed in 1919.

According to The Canadian Encyclopedia, "Prohibition was too short-lived in Canada to engender any real success. Opponents maintained that it violated British traditions of individual liberty, and that settling the matter by referendum or plebiscite was an aberration from Canadian parliamentary practice. Quebec rejected it as early at 1919. As a result, Quebec reaped huge profits from the sale of booze."

In 1920, British Columbia voted "wet," and by the following year some alcoholic beverages were legally sold there, and in the Yukon, through government stores. Manitoba inaugurated a system of government sale and control of alcohol in 1923, followed by Alberta and Saskatchewan in 1924, Newfoundland in 1925, Ontario and New Brunswick in 1927, and Nova Scotia in 1930. The last bastion, Prince Edward Island, gave up in 1948. Pockets of dryness, under local option, continued for years throughout the country.

The availability of alcohol often led to great shortages and beer parlours, private clubs, and liquor stores would close for several days at a time until the next shipment came in. This, in turn, led to binge drinking. The rationing of alcohol continued for many years after the Second World War.

Many senior Canadians recall the existence of segregated bars that existed across Canada. There was an entrance for men only and a separate one for "Ladies and Escorts." Few "nice" ladies went to bars; fewer still drank beer. Some women did drink at home, often alone, and in secrecy. Women were not permitted to drink in Legions until after the Second World War.

In the late 1950s many industries in the country were warning the government that there was a serious problem with alcohol consumption in the workforce. Some provincial governments became so alarmed by the problems that British Columbia, for example, banned certain people from buying alcohol. In 1963, 4,500 people were legally forbidden liquor in the province. Compulsory treatment for alcoholism was also under consideration.

The consumption of alcohol remains a problem today. Prohibition was originally enacted across Canada to insure the use of grain and fruit for supplies instead of use for raw materials for alcohol. No one could have imagined that this measure would eventually lead to overdrinking and addiction.

Those government regulations of liquor sales remain largely in effect. Most of the liquor purchased by residents of Ontario is from government-run stores operated by the Liquor Control Board of Ontario. The selection of those alcoholic beverages is solely controlled by the province. Right up until 2016, when some grocery stores were allowed to sell alcohol (albeit under tight legislation), the government refused to relinquish any control. Is that not akin to prohibition?

THE GREAT DEPRESSION

The Great Depression was a terrible time for Canadians. By 1933, almost one-third of all Canadian workers were out of a job. A legion of young men began "riding the rails." They hitched rides on railway box-cars to travel the country, to look for jobs that were not there. Except for a very small old-age-pension scheme, there was no social-welfare system. There was no unemployment insurance, no health care for the sick, no welfare for the poverty-stricken. By 1933, 800,000 Canadians — men, women, and children — were forced to ask private charities or governments for help.

The first expression for vouchers for food, boots, clothing, coal, and shelter was "pogey." It was a hardship for many people to ask for relief; some men cried when they needed to take it. "In the thirties, Canadians had their pride. Relief was a disgrace. Men would say that never in the history of their family — and they'd usually mention something about the British Empire Loyalists, or coming west with the first CPR trains — never had they had to go on relief," remarked one city relief officer.

"Our governments insisted that no one had the right to free hand-outs. The individual cannot … forever turn to the state to correct every misadventure which may befall him," said the cabinet minister in charge of relief grants.

Payments were kept lower than the lowest-paying jobs to discourage people from applying. It took at least seven dollars a week to feed a family of five in Ontario in 1932. In Toronto the weekly food allowance was

Courtesy of the Ontario Archives.

The Great Depression of the 1930s was a time when one-third of all Canadian workers were out of work. Men, women, and children were forced to beg for charity.

$6.93. The food allowance in Quebec was $3.25, and in Newfoundland it was six cents a day for each family member.

Some people appealed to Prime Minister Bennett, telling him of their troubles. "I am a married man, age twenty-six, with one child and have been working for the last three months for little more than my board and have had to break my home up. I am willing to do any kind of work for any length of time. I sincerely hope that you might have some kind of job that you could offer me so I can get my wife and child back."

Prime Minister Bennett had every letter answered. Some people found a five dollar bill stuffed in an envelope along with a reply from the prime minister.

Bennett was a self-made millionaire. He controlled the E.B. Eddy Paper Company. During his term as prime minister he never earned less than $150,000 a year. He disliked spending government money on relief programs and he truly believed that unemployment was not a major

Sam McLaughlin, founder of General Motors of Oshawa, sets a gas-saving example by giving up his car and returning to a horse and McLaughlin carriage.

problem. He once told a group of students that the greatest asset a person could have to spur them through life's trials was poverty.

The two-thirds of Canadians who still had jobs during the Depression saw it as a time of entertainment and an opportunity to make money through real estate investments. Dave Eaton, heir to the T. Eaton Company fortune, described the Depression as a time of fun and good times. Mr. Eaton said you could have a date to supper and a dance at a hotel for ten dollars. He felt it was a good time for everybody. Truth be told, the people with money and jobs had little sympathy for the poor and the unemployed.

"Drifters," homeless men on the move around the country, were considered a danger to the peace and safety of many communities. Prime Minister Bennett decided to create relief camps in the bush. Here the men were given food, shelter, army-style clothing, and twenty cents a day. In return they constructed bridges or roads and cut trees or dug ditches for public-works projects.

Courtesy of the Ontario Archives

A slum poorhouse in Toronto, circa 1900.

It was a restless time. Many citizens turned away from the two major political parties. The Liberal and Conservative parties supported hands-off economic policies, and neither wanted to tamper with the economic system.

It took the Second World War to stimulate the economic growth, to create jobs, to rally the people, and end the Great Depression.

ELDERS' CONFERENCE, 1992

This past weekend I attended the Aboriginal Elders' Conference held at Trent University in Peterborough. I discovered something about myself, and about Ontario.

This wasn't my first conference, nor would it be my last, and yet each conference always feels as though it is my first. I walked the corridors of the university and passed by many Aboriginal people. Some were dressed casually and others adorned with brilliant jewellery sparkling around their necks, and clothing in rich colours draped over their shoulders or around their waists. Some people were smiling and others stared straight ahead, intent on reaching their destination on time. I just seemed to float along, observing the crowds, catching the odd conversation and quietly blending in, as much as a white person can blend in, definitely not in colour, but in the natural spirit of the event.

Each year the Aboriginal peoples gather at Trent University to listen to their elders speak; to hear words of healing and the sound of sacred drums; to awaken to the heart song — the heartbeat of a sacred drum; to experience the past and the present together and open their eyes to the future.

The truth is the act of making a connection to tradition. We seem to lack this in our society. Everyone had this, at one time and place, but apparently it was lost when we immigrated to a new land, two centuries ago.

To attend an Aboriginal conference is to experience the historical heartbeat of the land, to view a clear picture of harmony with the elements and the emotional connection to Mother Earth; to embrace simplicity and awaken to respect for all things. In essence, such a conference is a spark of life and love, a cultural happening and an encompassment of all people.

We often talk about discovering this or that about Ontario, but what about the discovery of ourselves in Ontario? We need to awaken our own love of life and our care for others by awakening to a new consciousness of self-discovery.

During the course of the weekend I shared conversations with many people — Aboriginal and non-Aboriginal. These discussions explored who we were individually and collectively and how that knowledge could help us to help each other. It was emotional and personal.

Even shopping for art became a journey of exploration. People selected items not just for decoration but to help give purpose to their lives and to assist them to honour their paths of spiritual development. Artwork became medicine.

What the Aboriginal peoples want and inspire is a need for tradition — the need to share what we have, for growth. Can we, any of us, really own land? What, if anything, do we own? When all is said and done, we are gone on to something else. What we had belongs now to some other person. After all, you can't take it with you! We pay such a price for ownership.

When our forefathers arrived on this continent for a fresh start they brought with them this need for ownership. If we had abolished this attitude and created a system based on sharing, it would be a very different world today. An elders' conference would be a conference of continued wisdom and tradition, a future to behold.

NATURE IN VICTORIA COUNTY

Looking for that special place to spend a serene afternoon exploring nature? Victoria County has exactly what you are seeking. In fact, there are three conservation areas that are located within the county. Each of these areas is unique in itself, yet all of them provide facilities for a variety of outdoor activities that will allow you to experience the beauty and wonders of the natural world.

The Ken Reid Conservation Area, the smallest of the three areas, is only a five-minute drive north of Lindsay on Highway 35. Bordered on three sides by Sturgeon Lake, McLaren Creek, and Goose Bay, it consists of two trails that meander through a mixture of habitats, including open meadows, mixed forests, and wetlands. The facilities include picnic shelters, marsh boardwalks, a canoe launch, an observation platform, and a beach. During the winter months the trails are converted to cross-country skiing trails, which are suitable to all levels of experience.

The diversity of the natural habitats at the Ken Reid Conservation Area means the area is home to a large variety of plants and animals. An observant visitor out for a stroll could encounter a female Ruffed Grouse protecting her young, a rotund porcupine ambling among cedar trees, an Eastern Bluebird building its nest, or view the spectacular dive of an Osprey fishing for dinner.

The area is renowned for its large population of Osprey that nest in the neighbouring marshes and is believed to be the highest density of nesting Ospreys within Ontario.

The Pigeon River Headwaters Conservation Area is located approximately twenty-five kilometres south of Lindsay, southwest of the junction of Highways 35 and 7a, on McGill Road. It consists of 308 acres of mature deciduous forests, open meadows, and low-lying valley lands. This conservation area was acquired to protect the many coldwater streams and springs that serve to maintain the supply of water to the Pigeon River.

Most magnificent here at this conservation site are two large deciduous forests, which are home to century-old Sugar Maples and Black Cherry trees.

The Fleetwood Creek Natural Area is a nine hundred-acre tract of land managed by the Kawartha Region Conservation Authority for the Ontario Heritage Foundation. Located north of Pontypool, and within the geographic region known as the Oak Ridges Moraine, the area is characterized by steep valleys, lowland forests, coldwater streams, and adjacent wet meadows.

Courtesy of the Ontario Archives.

Elegant ladies enjoying nature on a Sunday afternoon.

An observation platform at the edge of the valley offers a terrific view of the surrounding area at any time of the year. You can watch a rainstorm move in, a mist rise from the cold streams, or admire a fresh snowfall.

Within the boundaries of the park 268 species of flora have been identified, and at least forty-four species of birds, including a population of re-introduced wild turkeys.

Wherever you go, nature has something to offer. Go and get it.

MEMORIES OF ONTARIO

In 1979, I wrote a book entitled *Under This Roof: Old Homesteads of Ontario*, published by Doubleday. In 1987, *Memories of Ontario* appeared in bookstores across Ontario, published by Canon Books. Many people queried me about the span of time between books.

Writing a book is a thoughtful creation. There is a canvas in your mind and a brush (pen) in your hand. The picture is painted in words inspired by your feeling towards the time and events you wish to portray. The concept and presentation is influenced by the current market and must appeal to a publisher. That requires research and diligence to get your canvas on the wall.

Memories of Ontario was a unique concept, considering what the book entailed. For example, it reveals that the community of Oakville was once the site of an Aboriginal village, as were Burlington, Hamilton, London, and St. Catharines. St. Catharines was once home to one of the largest Aboriginal burial grounds in North America, covering several acres of land.

Many exciting photographs from back as far as the 1860s depict not only the Aboriginal people, but the early pioneers who came here to begin new lives. The book followed the settlement of the French in Ontario as well as the United Empire Loyalists. *Memories of Ontario* told the story behind the villages, towns, and cities of Ontario. Several chapters highlighted the unusual stories of Ontario history, such as shipwrecks, Aboriginal war chiefs, inventors, explorers, and the women

Stan Richmond's boat, the *Shebeskekong,* is picking up a car to take out to an island near Parry Sound.

Ivan Hunt, the author's father-in-law, stands by his new Chevrolet in Noble, Ontario.

who founded villages and fought side by side with their husbands in the War of 1812.

I endeavoured to capture the true spirit of the land as it was prior to early settlement based on written accounts of early explorers. The forests stood strong and reached upward to touch blue sky above. Pioneers needed to clear the land to see sunlight, blocked out as it was by the dense woods. Within a short time, the land was transformed.

The story of change and progress was recorded in detail in *Memories of Ontario*. Loss of life and loss of natural environment can be seen in the 147 photographs in that book.

Memories of Ontario was designed to take the reader on a journey from early history to the present time. Local folklore also gives reasons why various settlements were situated where they were.

Memories of Ontario was a book you could take with you on your travels throughout Ontario. As you turned the pages, you would turn many corners of historical significance.

THE BROUGHAM APPLE BASKET

In the tiny hamlet of Kinsale, located just north of Ajax, lives a fine and dedicated craftsman. His name is Ken Spratley. The craft he is known for throughout Canada is basket making.

The basket industry that relates to the Brougham Apple Basket dates back to 1866. Two men by the name of Fennell and Wilkinson operated a mill located in the village of Brougham. The owners of the mill produced brooms, paint brush handles, barrels, and a variety of mechanically manufactured containers used by local farmers and growers for picking, gathering, and storing produce and fruit.

In 1874, William Barnes bought out the factory and hired Bill Pennock to run the mill. In 1896, Mr. Pennock designed the oval, round bottom Brougham apple basket. Up to that time most baskets used in picking were square bottomed. Once the basket was loaded with apples it had to be dumped into larger containers for transportation to market.

Square baskets when dumped tended to hold up apples, and when released they would bump and bruise. This greatly reduced their market value and caused spoilage during long-term storage.

Bill Pennock came to the rescue. Using known manufacturing techniques, he designed a new half-bushel basket that utilized the same skills, experience, building techniques, and materials that are used today to produce the standard bushel basket. Local growers lined the inside with burlap to further protect the fruit and to facilitate the gentle unloading of rolling apples. Runners were eventually added to the bottom for strength and longer life. The resulting design has no gaps, unlike woven baskets. Three pounds of hardwood goes into building a large half-bushel basket. Dependent on availability, elm, maple, and ash have been, and still are, used today to construct the basket.

In 1924, William Barnes died. His factory was sold to the White brothers. During the flood of 1929, the factory was destroyed. Old Frank Pennock bought the Doulton factory, located on the Postel side road, and began operations anew.

During the 1950s, Norm Kristianson bought the factory. With a declining market and worn out equipment the factory struggled on.

In 1972, at the request of his wife, who was teaching crafts, Ken Spratley visited Norm Kristianson to purchase baskets. However, Kristianson was unable to keep up the production and the final order never materialized. By 1973, the factory was expropriated for the infamous Pickering Airport. Spratley approached Kristianson to learn how to make the Brougham Apple Basket.

Although Ken did manage to acquire some of the original basket moulds, he had to work out many of the construction details himself. He even invented a staining method that used, caught and re-used his black-walnut, hand-made stain.

In 1978, Ken went into full production making both small and half-bushel size baskets. Annually, he produces four thousand baskets.

Thanks to Ken Spratley a Canadian craft and tradition continues, and I even own a couple of them, I am proud to say.

BANCROFT ROCK FESTIVAL

On the Civic Holiday weekend in 1988, I attended the 25th Anniversary of the Bancroft Rockhound Gemboree. The show was held in the North Hastings Community Centre in Bancroft.

The Rockhound Gemboree featured thirty-five mineral dealers, some having attended the show since its beginning in 1963.

On Thursday morning, I paid my thirteen-dollar entrance fee, and proceeded on a walking tour of the show. The first stop was outside at the swapping tables where, for trade dollars, one could purchase stones from the many collectors and prospectors who had brought the best of their collections. The individuals behind the tables were as interesting as the stones they were selling or trading. Imagine what it would be like to carry a knapsack on your back, pick in hand, and scour a mountain of earth to dig a gem. I was so caught up in the show, I even purchased a five dollar ticket on a draw for a canoe. I am still waiting to hear if I won.

In the arena itself there were rows and rows of tables laden with gemstones, fossils, beads, and jewellery. One exhibitor was selling prehistoric mammoth ribs from Florida. The dealer asked me if I was interested in prehistoric fossils and then promptly presented me with two boxes to open. The boxes were full of bones — a dinosaur tail. Although he tried to sell me that tail, I resisted.

I was amazed at the beauty of the stones — the opals, amethysts, quartz crystals, and even a rock on display that had been brought back from the moon by one of the astronauts.

In conjunction with the show, there were guided field trips, done by the Central Canadian Federation of Mineralogical Societies. "Field trippers," as they are called, assemble at the Gemboree and pay a nominal fee to participate in a day of fun and discovery. An added attraction was Dr. Donald Gorman, from the University of Toronto, who was on hand throughout the Gemboree to examine and identify any minerals collected. This was a complimentary service provided by the Ministry of Natural Resources.

The Bancroft Rockhound Gemboree runs each year on Civic Holiday weekend, starting on Thursday and continuing until Sunday.

Of note, since 1988 it has grown to fill two buildings and has some stone carving available to be observed.

Courtesy of the Ontario Archives.

BANCROFT, ONT.

Bancroft, the mineral capital of Canada, circa 1915.

DEMOGRAPHICS

Demographics is a keyword today. It plays a critical role in a nation's economy and social structure. The more we are able to understand demographic realities, the better we will be able to cope with them. These studies and statistics are a world of discovery. They provide us with the opportunity to truly understand trends and movements in Ontario and in the rest of the country.

In 1996, David K. Foote, an economist at the University of Toronto, and Daniel Stoffman, an award-winning journalist and former graduate of the London School of Economics, published a book called *Boom, Bust and Echo*. It was a very informative piece of literature revealing past patterns in society and indicating some future directions in Ontario, and in the country.

The book described the baby-boomer generation, those born between 1947 and 1966. This generation of people has changed the economy, driven housing construction, as well as other markets, and transformed many social attitudes and lifestyle choices. For example, in 1985 tennis was booming in Canada. Clubs had waiting lists and public courts were crowded, even on weekdays. As the 1990s progressed, something unexpected happened: the waiting lists evaporated at the tennis clubs. According to Foote, "Those who oversee and promote the sport have expressed bewilderment. They shouldn't be surprised. What has happened to tennis was predictable. Because of the combination of low fertility rate and increasing life expectancy the

Canadian population is aging, which means simply that the average age of Canadians is increasing. And older people do not play tennis as much as young people."

According to the demographic shift, bird watching and hiking will become a main pastime for the boomers. In the United States today, 65 million birdwatchers are spending 5.2 billion dollars annually on bird-related products.

"Canada's 9.8 million baby-boomers begin turning fifty years of age in 1997. This means the travel industry will reap the benefits," adds Foote. Tourism will be a growth industry. People in their late forties and fifties will seek out peace and quiet. People will appreciate nature and they're in the market for something new, like digging for dinosaur bones in Alberta, visiting the shores of Lake Superior, or snorkelling off a small island in the Pacific. Of course, all of this has to be paid for somehow.

By 1992, lottery sales nationwide were 1.7 billion dollars a year. According to Foote, people are most likely to afford recreation in their forties and fifties. And that is when they start buying lottery tickets and visiting casinos.

"An Italian politician once argued that lotteries were a bad public policy because they encouraged people to gamble away money that was needed to feed, house, and clothe their families. Canada, it seems, has a plentiful supply of apparent idiots.

"Many of the baby-boomers in the coming years are going to be semi-retired, like working three days a week for sixty percent of their salary. We will need to redefine pension systems and economic systems so we can better accommodate the needs of Canada's aging society. Of Canada's working-age population, of 15 to 64, some 42.4 percent are 45 or older, the vast majority of them baby boomers," states Foote.

The traditional retirement age of sixty-five was established in Germany in 1916, during an era when life expectancy was significantly lower. A 2012 report from the Canadian Institute for Health Information found that far fewer Canadians die before the age of seventy-five than they did thirty years ago. Demographics show us an average life expectancy of eighty-one years. Canadians are living, and working, longer. Baby boomers continue to spell change for the workplace and communities at large. This has a large ripple-effect on our youth — fewer opportunities and higher stress levels. We need to take some action to address the new demographics that are emerging.

SHIPWRECK

One of the most interesting chapters of Ontario history involve shipwrecks, and some of the greatest shipwrecks were in the Georgian Bay area.

Many ships left the safety of the Owen Sound harbour, never to return again. Such was the case of the steamer *Asia*, built in St. Catharines in 1873.

The story began near midnight on September 13, 1882, as the steamer *Asia* cruised out of the harbour at Owen Sound, bound for Sault Ste. Marie, with more than a hundred passengers on board. There were only two survivors: Christina Morrison of Owen Sound and Douglas Tinkis of Little Current.

Laden with eighty-five tons of merchandise and fifteen horses tethered to the deck of her hull, she cut a smooth path across the water's edge. It was a clear night with a gentle, warm breeze out of the southwest when, steady on her course, the *Asia* headed out of the sound.

The night passed without difficulty. By morning a stiff westerly gale had begun to blow and Captain Savage changed his course and ran before the wind. He headed for the French River, but the ship wasn't fast enough to outrun the storm. The horses, sensing danger, frantically scrambled to break away from the railings. Orders went out to throw the animals and as much cargo as possible overboard. Passengers scurried to the deck wearing life preservers.

Awakened by his uncle, Douglas Tinkis jumped from his bunk and scrambled to the deck. Mr. Tinkis remembered it like this: "This storm was raging, the wind blowing a perfect hurricane and the waves appeared to be

Christina Morrison of Owen Sound was one of two survivors of the sinking of the steamer *Asia* in September of 1882.

The *Asia*, laden with eighty-five tons of merchandise before it left the harbour of Owen Sound bound for Sault Ste. Marie. The ship never made it to its destination.

rolling mountains high. The steamer had got into the trough of the sea and though her engines worked hard, the vessel refused to obey her helmsman. Wave after wave swept over us, each of which threatened to engulf us, until one, larger than the rest struck us, and the ship turned on its side."

Miss Morrison had risen about 8 a.m. on the morning of the 14th, but because she felt seasick she returned to her cabin. She stated: "I knew there was danger, and I saw people putting on life preservers. My state room was about in the middle of the ship on the port side, my cabin door opened out on deck. At about 11 a.m. the ship appeared to take a violent lurch to starboard. I climbed up over the ship, which was sinking rapidly, and let myself slide down into the water. The captain and mate assisted me into a lifeboat."

Mr. Tinkis also managed to haul himself into the lifeboat. He recalled, "As soon as I got in I looked towards the wreck, where nothing was to be seen but a struggling mass of humanity, who were clinging to pieces of timber and other wreckage to prolong their lives even for a few seconds."

Three life boats drifted for a short time. Soon two of the boats disappeared in the trough of a hurling wave to later reappear, empty of its passengers.

A fleet of ships docked in Parry Sound.

With no land in view, the eighteen survivors of the *Asia* valued every breath. With every wave, the numbers diminished. The struggle for life had begun. One by one, passengers disappeared in the waves.

Despite the agony around them, Miss Morrison and Douglas Tinkis remained firm. Two days later the two of them reached land, about forty kilometres from Parry Sound. Everyone else had perished. Local Aboriginals helped them into Parry Sound.

And this is just one of the many shipwreck stories of Georgian Bay.

A YOUNG BRIDE'S DREAM

The Beatty family of Parry Sound were involved in shipping on Georgian Bay. They owned a steamship business called the Beatty Lines and were pioneers in the Canadian shipping industry. Tragedy befell their shipping lines early one winter day in 1879. The eerie and mysterious tragedy was also the last voyage of the steamer *Waubuno* and had been foretold by the last dream of a young bride of only three weeks.

The *Waubuno* was built by the Beatty Ship Lines in 1865 at Port Robinson, and it was the beginning of their fame on the upper lakes. The hull was towed to Collingwood the same year and there the machinery was installed. The *Waubuno* was also the beginning of Canada Steamship Lines and Canadian Pacific Steamships.

For years, the *Waubuno*, a two-hundred-ton wooden sidewheeler, made weekly trips between Parry Sound and Collingwood, carrying freight and passengers during the flourishing shipping trade on Lake Huron and Georgian Bay. For the Beatty family this lucrative business was heaven-sent, until a young bride of three weeks had a dream — a premonition of death.

On the evening of November 20, 1879, Mrs. Doupe, the new bride, and her husband, a doctor, retired for the night. They were to make their way from Collingwood to Parry Sound in just two days time and from there to the village of McKeller, a few kilometres north of the town. There Dr. Doupe would take up the practice of medicine. That night, however, Mrs. Doupe saw the *Waubuno* beset with gigantic waves in her dreams.

The *Waubuno*, a two-hundred-ton wooden sidewheeler, travelled between Parry Sound and Collingwood in the 1870s.

She and her husband, along with the other passengers, were struggling in the waters for their lives. She had foreseen her own death. Would they still board the ship?

The next day, news of her dream spread to the captain, the crew, and other passengers of the vessel. Although the story became a joke in Collingwood, many passengers opted not to sail in the face of this foreboding premonition.

Of that fateful day, David William, editor of the *Collingwood Enterprise Bulletin*, wrote, "Saturday, November 22, 1879, was a wild and winter-like day. The wind blew and snow squalls were frequent. All the previous day it had been blowing great guns, and the *Waubuno* lay at the dock in Collingwood with one of the largest loads of the season, a number of passengers, a crew of 14, and all were waiting for the gale to abate sufficiently for her to start for Parry Sound."

Neither gale nor a bride's dream was going to stop Captain Burkett, master of the *Waubuno*, from setting sail. Besides, the captain was eyeing the *Maganettawan*, a new ship put into service the same year by the Georgian Bay Lumber Company. It was lying across the harbour, loaded and ready to sail. The *Maganettawan* had beat the *Waubuno* on so many impromptu races along the north shore that Captain Burkett was determined not be out-sailed this time.

At 4:00 a.m. on November 22, the 150-foot steamboat silently sailed out of Collingwood without even a toot of its whistle to notify anyone of its departure. The gale, which had been blowing "great guns" for two days, had moderated. The trip to Parry Sound was short and relatively safe, normally, except for a thirty-two-kilometre stretch between Hope Island and Lone Rock, where boats were exposed to open waters.

The bride and her husband had no chance to protest, since they were both asleep in their cabin when the *Waubuno* headed out. The ship was later sighted, on schedule, by John Hoar, the lighthouse keeper on Christian Island. At noon, the *Waubuno* whistle was heard repeatedly by lumberjacks at Moon River. By then a heavy snowstorm was blowing, but no one thought anything of it. The ship often stopped for a whistle-pick-up of passengers among the islands. No one suspected that the *Waubuno* was in trouble.

Apparently, when Captain Burkett came to the end of the northern leg of the course, at Lone Rock, he ran into a blinding snow storm and sixty-four-kilometre-an-hour winds. Unable to obtain a clear sighting on Lone Rock, he dared not turn into the narrow western entrance of Waubuno Channel.

At that point the captain turned back and headed for the gap among the islands between Moose Deer Point and Copperhead. Although his navigation was on the nose, he had no way to know of an uncharted shoal in the middle of his projected passage. Normally this shoal was six metres down, but the southwest gale had changed all that. Seeing sprouting breakers here, the captain dropped anchors, but the anchors did not catch. Years later, divers found a small anchor lying loose on the bottom and a larger anchor standing straight up, with five turns of anchor chain around the stock. The ship had shifted and come to rest and held. There, the *Waubuno* tossed in the breakers. It was only a question of time before something gave. Hence the distress signals. Suddenly, the foredeck gave way, the anchor was loose, and the ship was back in the gale. Downwind was an exposed rock and the paddle-wheeler hit it — hard. The engine-room machinery went to the bottom, the flotation hull ended up at Wreck Island, the ship split lengthwise, and everything went down.

No survivors and no bodies were ever found. All of the life preservers were later discovered among the wreckage, but no bodies. Why were the passengers not wearing life preservers, and what happened to them? It was a tragedy, and a mysterious one at that.

THE PARANORMAL
AND THE UNEXPLAINED

THE MYSTERIES OF LONG POINT

Long Point is a naturalist's paradise. On one side it has marsh areas, and on the other side it has sand dunes. The marsh areas provide a habitat for about three hundred species of birds and their seasonal migration delights many birdwatchers.

Long Point Park is a sand spit that juts out into Lake Erie. It is by no means fixed or stable. The land and water continually change and shift. A geographer once remarked, "We can expect the north shore of Lake Erie to continue to erode at an average rate of twenty-five feet per year to the westward of Long Point until it eventually stabilizes in or about the town of Tillsonburg, presently twenty miles inland."

As early as 1000 C.E. Aboriginal peoples roamed the Long Point region. During the fur-trading days an unscrupulous trader by the name of David Ramsey conducted business in the Long Point area. Ramsey enticed Aboriginal people to his trading post by promising them an ample supply of rum. It was reported, on at least one occasion, that Ramsey killed and scalped three Aboriginal people during a drinking binge. From that day forward Ramsey lurked about in fear.

In 1790, he and two of his cohorts left Detroit with a cargo of prime furs and a considerable amount of gold. While camping at Port Stanley they were confronted by a group of Aboriginal people who wanted Ramsey to supply them with some rum. He refused and broke camp. The Aboriginal people followed him all the way to Long Point. Fearing for the loss of his gold if overtaken by the Aboriginal people, Ramsey decided to bury his treasure. He set the chest laden with gold into a shallow hole in the ground.

As a further precaution, he killed a black dog and put the body onto the chest before filling the hole in with sand so that the chest would be even less visible if stumbled upon. He never did return. Local lore claims that the chest of money remains buried somewhere on Long Point.

Also in 1790, John Troyer, a botanist who was very knowledgeable about medicinal properties of flora, settled at Long Point. Troyer was unusually gifted with second sight and also had the ability to divine for metals and water. He was well respected by his neighbours for his ability to work with medicine and was known as Dr. Troyer. Other neighbours considered him to be a witch doctor.

Over time Dr. Troyer became paranoid. He was sure that he was being persecuted by witches. He attributed his mental and physical pains to evil spells cast over him by sinister hags.

In his book entitled *Lore and Legends of Long Point*, Henry D. Barrett described Dr. Troyer's fears and activities. "As he grew older his terror of them [witches] grew to the point where he bolted a large bear trap to the floor at the foot of his bed and set it nightly to deter them."

Despite this, the doctor claimed that, on occasion, he was taken from his home — by witches.

Barrett adds, "He often related how he had been snatched from a peaceful sleep, turned into a horse and ridden by his tormentors across Lake Erie to Dunkirk, New York, where they attended a clandestine dance."

Eventually, despite the witches, the doctor used his gift of divination to search for Ramsey's lost chest of gold. He set out one night, with a candle in one hand and a bible in the other. His son Michael accompanied him. Exploring the sand dunes he eventually pinpointed the location of the chest. He directed his son to dig. At the stroke of midnight Michael's shovel struck metal. He dropped to his knees and frantically began to scrape the sand from the top of the steel chest, slowly prying open the lid. Just as the black dog was being revealed a strong current of air suddenly extinguished their candle and they fled the scene, never to return.

Some years later, two young men enticed by local lore conceived the idea that the chest of gold had been buried with the good doctor. One night they decided to dig up the grave of Dr. Troyer. Barrett described what happened next. "As this pair of ghouls were lifting the doctor's bones from the collapsed coffin, there was a sudden rush of wind over their heads. On looking up, they were terrified to see a huge white bird, with fiery red eyes and a fiercely snapping beak, swooping down upon them. Their exploration ended abruptly, never to be resumed."

There are no more stories of the buried treasure on Long Point, but many other mysteries endure. A wealthy American who fled Port Rowan after the American Revolution was rumoured to have buried a large sum of money and other valuables along Squires Ridge on Long Point. Nothing, so far, has surfaced.

William Porritt, a lighthouse keeper and guide, witnessed a few things, including shipwrecks. He even buried a few of the shipwrecked sailors in the 1880s, and according to him no plants would grow on their gravesites and the beach sand turned red for a year over all the graves.

At times a headless seaman has been seen moaning on the shore. Legend has it that he fell head first and was decapitated when lowering a rescue boat from a grounded schooner. Chock-a-block with myth, legend, treasure, birds, and shifting sands, Long Point is worthy of a stay!

STRANGE CREATURES
SWIMMING IN OUR WATERS

Old legends and tales, as recounted by early explorers and settlers, speak of strange creatures living in Lake Ontario and some other bodies of water.

Pierre Raddison, a famous French explorer, noted an abundance of large, "aquatic serpents" in Ontario's waters. A German scientist, along on an expedition in the 1700s, wrote an entire paper on the subject. In August of 1829, a very large water snake, six to nine metres in length with a head that was twenty-five to thirty-five centimetres in diameter, was recorded at a beach near St. Catharines. In 1835, the crew and passengers of a schooner sighted a three-metre-long serpent as round as a flour barrel, dark blue and spotted brown, with a small head, swimming in the Kingston harbour.

The *British Whig* newspaper featured an article on August 29, 1867, on the super-abundance of mysterious aquatic monsters of the strangest and most unheard-of descriptions. It also indicated that many of the residents, living along the shores of the Great Lakes, were well aware of them!

Charleston Lake, in eastern Ontario, was, for many years, considered to be a fisherman's paradise and a summer vacation favourite for people from as far away as Pennsylvania. This lake is fourteen kilometres long and six kilometres wide; its waters, clear and cold, are more than one hundred and thirty-seven metres deep.

The lake is carved out of the Frontenac Axis, a relatively narrow extension of the Canadian Shield bedrock, which dominates the landscape of Northern Ontario. The lake is the principal watershed for the Gananoque River. A few miles to the west and east are lowlands that once formed the floor of an ancient sea. In that ancient sea prehistoric monsters apparently swam.

A strange creature, nicknamed Charlie by local residents, has been sighted repeatedly over the past hundred years in Charleston Lake. In 1897, Noah Shook claimed he was pursued by a large, hissing creature. In 1947, three fishermen reported that they had seen a dinosaur-like creature swimming at Tallow Bay Rock. In 1997, a couple boating on the lake at night claimed they saw waves that were one to two metres high, caused by something swimming in the water.

A snake-like creature has been sighted living in Red Horse Lake, near Lyndhurst. The creature is said to be greenish black, a head like a horse, with small breathing tubes on its head. It is estimated to be between eighteen and twenty-four metres in length.

Giant snakes have also been reported in Shingleton Lake. Area residents once found a nesting spot under some brush where a three-metre circle had been pressed down, much in the same manner as a snake might do.

One such snake was tracked through the snow where it had left a trail the size of a stovepipe with evidence of small feet along the side. It climbed to the top of a hill where, on the other side, there was a six-metre drop to the water. From the marks left in the snow, it was apparently long enough to reach down to the open water while keeping part of its body on the hill.

These three lakes — Charleston, Red Horse, and Shingleton — are in close proximity.

In Muskrat Lake, at Cobden, Ontario, a strange creature was reported as early as 1916 and as late as 1977. It has been described as having three eyes, three ears, a big fin halfway down its back, two legs, and one large tooth in front; it is silvery-green in colour and stretches for seven metres.

At Fraser Lake near Bancroft, in September 1925, a two-metre alligator attacked and bit a young girl. Hunters found its tracks on the lakeshore and riverbanks for several years thereafter.

In August 1952, three fishermen heard a strange hissing sound while fishing on a lake at Conway Marsh near Palmer Rapids. To their surprise, they saw a strange creature circle the boat, and then disappear. They described it as "ten feet long with black skin."

Legends and tales or fact … you decide!

STRANGE LIGHTS IN THE SKY

For centuries there have been reports of strange lights in the sky, strange crafts landing on earth, and even of living creatures emerging from these spaceships. In recent years more of these craft sightings have been reported to the authorities. Most of them are easily explained away, but some completely defy explanation.

Numerous historical stories have reported about strange apparitions in the sky. Yet, it was only after the Second World War that these sightings first attracted serious attention.

It all began on June 24, 1947. Kenneth Arnold reported seeing a formation of gleaming discs flying over the Rocky Mountains. He described them as "skipping like saucers across water," and the name flying saucer quickly captured the public imagination. An official investigation adopted the more cautious name of "Unidentified Flying Object."

UFO spotting is nothing new, but the recording of reports is. Many early UFO reports came from monasteries, which were places of learning. On January 1, 1254, a mysterious coloured flying saucer appeared in England. Its presence was recorded by monks.

In London, England, on December 11, 1741, at 9:45 p.m. a small, oval ball of fire descended and at a height of about eight hundred metres, levelled off, and headed eastward.

On September 7, 1820, a stream of saucer-shaped objects crossed a town in France while flying in formation. While over the town, the objects changed course and made a perfect ninety-degree turn, keeping to their strict formation.

In 1951, a circular, bright orange-red disk was observed by the pilot of the U.S. Navy R5D four-engine transport, cruising 3,000 metres over the North Atlantic, enroute from Iceland to Newfoundland. This sighting is dubbed the Gander UFO Case.

One of the most famous UFO events is the so-called Washington Invasion. On the summer evening of July 19, 1952, the citizens of the United States capital were treated to a display of five strong lights, which manoeuvred for hours over the White House, the city, and the countryside.

A week later, the lights reappeared. One F94 jet was sent in pursuit. The pilot radioed in that he was approaching a cluster of huge blue and white lights. As he closed in the lights moved to form a ring around him and travelled along with him for about fifteen seconds before moving away.

On July 20, 1957, a glowing, domed object was observed to hover over a field for the better part of an hour before taking off near Galt, Ontario. Military investigators later discovered a nine-metre circle of wilted grass, branches that were broken off a nearby tree, and three-toed footprints.

In May of 1967, mechanic Steven Michalak made physical contact with two UFOs at Whiteshell Provincial Park in Manitoba. The experience provided a wealth of detailed evidence. The encounter is known as the Falcon Lake Sighting.

Michalak was on a geological trek in the bush when he saw two cigar-shaped objects with humps on them about halfway down from the sky. As the objects came closer to earth they became more oval-shaped.

John Robert Colombo, in his book entitled *True Canadian UFO Stories*, states what happened next to Michalak. "Suddenly the farthest of the two objects — farthest from my point of vision — stopped dead in the air while its companion slipped down closer and closer to the ground and landed squarely on the flat top of a rock about 150 feet away from me."

Michalak added that he noticed an opening near the top of the craft and a brilliant purple light pouring out of the aperture. The light hurt his eyes. As he approached the object he could hear voices that sounded like humans. Standing in front of the craft, Michalak decided to have a look inside the opening of the ship. He described seeing a maze of lights.

"Direct beams running in horizontal and diagonal paths and a series of flashing lights, it seemed to me, were working in a random fashion, with no particular order or sequence. I took note of the thickness of the walls of the craft. They were about 20 inches thick at the cross-section."

Then the craft suddenly tilted slightly leftward, then rose above the treetops. It began to change colour and shape, following its sister ship. Soon the flying saucers were gone without a trace.

The date was October 24, 1967, at 4:00 a.m., in St. Catharines. Police constables Roger Willey and Clifford Waycott were on routine night duty in their patrol car when they suddenly saw bright lights in the shape of a large cross pulsating in the sky ahead of them. As the patrol car drove towards it, the object moved silently away. The policemen pursued it, but the object of light always managed to accelerate away from them.

Oscar Magocsi, a radio technologist, experienced a series of UFO sightings and eventually made contact outside Huntsville. He claimed he was transported to other worlds on September 21, 1974. He later published *My Space Odyssey in UFOs*.

On February 1, 1997, in Whitefish, Ontario, a man was up watching sports on television until 12:40 a.m. when he noticed a yellow light coming through the kitchen window. When he looked out the window, he noticed two quarter-moon-shaped objects hovering about one hundred feet in the air over the neighbour's property. The objects quickly vanished.

Have you ever seen a strange unexplainable light or object in the sky? Or are you like me, still sitting outside on a summer night beneath a northern sky waiting to see that unidentified flying object?

THE DISCOVERY OF THE CRYSTAL SKULL

The year was 1919; the place, British Honduras. The event was the discovery of an ancient citadel, the largest to have been found in the New World. It was discovered by Mike Mitchell-Hedges, an English explorer-archaeologist who named the site the City of Fallen Stones. Mitchell-Hedges had been granted a seven-year archaeological licence by the British Honduras government.

Shortly after the discovery, Mitchell-Hedges returned to England for supplies and further funding, but left his Canadian-adopted daughter, Anna, in the care of a local Maya Kekchi indigenous family. Upon his return in 1923, work started on the archaeological dig of the citadel. It was during this time that Anna's attention was captured by rays of brilliant, glittering, reflected sunlight as she wandered in the ruins of the temple. She rushed back to her father to tell him of the light. One by one the giant stone slabs were carefully removed as the crew sought to reveal the glitter in the rubble. It wasn't until January 1, 1924, the day of Anna's seventeenth birthday, that the final slab was lifted clear. Anna had discovered a crystal skull the size of a human head.

As Mitchell-Hedges held up the skull for all to see, the Maya Kekchi workers went wild with joy. Laughing and crying they kissed the ground and hugged each other. An ancient memory had been triggered.

The skull was a masterpiece, made from clear quartz. Who among the ancient people of the Americas could have possessed such knowledge and skill? Or had the skull come, as Mitchell-Hedges believed, from a civilization more ancient even than the Mayans? Some people called the object the Crystal Skull of Doom, somehow linked to death. Mitchell-Hedges and Anna claimed that the skull had a power that created such a mystique.

Three months later the detachable lower jaw of the Crystal Skull was also discovered, as whole and as perfect as the rest. The skull measures 124 millimetres wide, 147 millimetres high, 197 millimetres long, and its weight is five and one-half kilograms.

For the next three years the dig progressed, and the Crystal Skull remained in the possession of the Maya Kekchi. When the expedition prepared to depart for good, the Maya Kekchi people were sorry to see them go. Mitchell-Hedges had provided the people with modern medicine and physicians. To show their love and appreciation, the chief and his medicine man presented Mitchell-Hedges with their most treasured possession, the Crystal Skull.

Anna Mitchell-Hedges eventually settled in Southern Ontario. I recall the time I went to visit her, and there, sitting between us on the table in the living room, was the Crystal Skull. The skull was as clear as glass. You could see your own image in its face. Anna explained to me that whenever the skull is photographed a number of images appear, faces of people from another time. Is my image now captured in the skull?

Frank Dorland, an art restorer based in San Francisco who Anna loaned the skull to for many years, experienced visionary phenomena through the use of the skull. It was reported that he was fascinated by the skull's "aura." He heard what he took as the sound of faint high metallic bells, chimes, and other noises apparently emanating from the skull. He heard human voices softly singing strange chants. He talked about how the first time he kept the skull in his residence overnight there was the sound of a prowling jungle cat within his home, as well as the ringing of chimes and bells. He also found that the skull channeled lights from its base into the eye sockets, creating an awesome effect.

In March of 1962, *Fate Magazine* published an article written by John Sinclair entitled "Crystal Skull of Doom." It was a story detailing some anecdotes about the terrible things that had happened to people who make fun of the skull. One account sited a Zulu witch doctor who, in 1949, reportedly spat at the skull and performed a mockery dance at it. He was subsequently killed in a hut by a lightning flash out of a single cloud in a formerly cloudless sky. A news photographer visiting the skull shortly after the witch doctor's death willed the skull to kill him. Upon leaving the Mitchell-Hedges abode, he drove straight into a truck, killing himself. In addition, a woman reporter who had belittled the skull perished by a mysterious infection leading to heart failure.

Mark Chorvinsky with Douglas Chapman in their article "The Mitchell-Hedges Skull," cited a further account of death associated with the skull. "*Psychic* magazine mentioned that in the early 1950s three women died mysteriously after each had spent time viewing the skull.

"Anna Mitchell-Hedges related some intriguing accounts. One was about how Adrian Conan Doyle (the son of the creator of Sherlock Holmes) became very edgy when the skull was around, even if out of sight, and could ascertain its presence when he was visiting Anna. Another story concerned a neighbour's butler who felt the skull to be an ominous presence dominating Anna Mitchell-Hedges house."

Looking back on it now, I wonder who shone more, the Crystal Skull or Anna Mitchell-Hedges. I do know my experience with the Crystal Skull will remain with me always. And I did not die from viewing and holding it.

THE AGAWA PICTOGRAPHS OF LAKE SUPERIOR

The Agawa Pictographs are in a very sacred place. One hundred and forty-four kilometres north of Sault Ste. Marie on the rocky shoreline of Lake Superior stands a natural cathedral of stone. The entire Agawa area is part of Lake Superior Provincial Park, completely skirted by a deep bay and several miles of fine sand and gravel beaches. Here, at the Agawa River mouth, Ojibwa families have set up camp for thousands of years. The Ojibwa of the Agawa band inhabited one or two main villages throughout the various historical periods. These village sites were located at Sinclair Cove and near the Agawa River mouth.

Agawa Rock is an impressive and haunting spot, a sheer rock that rises high and towers above the cold, clear waters of Lake Superior. It is a spiritual place of ancient rock paintings. Some Aboriginal medicine people believe that the vertical cliffs are powerful places because the earth's energies are exposed.

The ancient rock paintings or pictographs, as they are called, are the work of Ojibwa shaman artists. These medicine people handled spiritual matters, conducted rituals, and worked to provide a link between this world and the spirit world.

Archeologists believe the art at Agawa Rock dates back three thousand years. They can deduce this from knowledge of the water levels of Lake Superior in relation to the pictographs prior to three thousand years ago.

The rock art represents the end product of religious experiences such as vision quests, group ceremonies, and the acknowledgement of spiritual assistance.

In 1990, Julie and Thor Conway, an archaeologist/anthropologist team, worked with two Ojibwa medicine people from the Garden River band. Together they documented the information presented in their book, *Spirit on Stone*.

Julia and Thor shared these findings: "Many of the pictograph site names refer to birds of prey. Each of the named sites is a vertical cliff dropping into a lake. When we pursued this lead, we found that shamans regarded large nesting birds, living atop cliffs, as metaphors for the presence of unseen thunderbirds."

Over a period of seventeen years, 117 paintings were recorded. One painting, showing a faint Thunderbird, was discovered as late as 1989.

In such a magnificent area we are reminded of the beauty of our natural heritage, and the need for preservation and appreciation for sacred spaces as well as the creation of new ones.

The present-day interest in Aboriginal culture reflects a deep need in our society for a renewal of the sense of the sacred.

BEYOND THE GRAVE

In 1934, three weeks after the death of her father, a young woman in Orillia had her first glimpse "beyond the veil."

She was alone in the house, relaxing in the living room with a good book, when she heard a sound. Surprised and, yes, startled, she realized it was the sound of dishes rattling. She got up to investigate and as she approached the hallway she caught sight of her father coming down the stairs with a tray of dishes.

She saw him very clearly, exactly as he had been in life, and heard herself exclaim, "Dad, what are you doing?"

Without a word, he smiled at her and vanished. Her first thought was to wonder how a tray of dishes, which had made such a clear clinking sound, could simply disappear into thin air. At no time did she feel frightened.

On another occasion, when she was working in the kitchen, she looked up to see him standing in the doorway. This time she did not speak. She thought perhaps the sound of her voice had made him vanish on his previous visit. For several minutes they stood looking at each other. She noticed he was wearing the cap that he had always worn in the house. Then, when she thought perhaps now she could speak, he disappeared once more. She never saw him again and often wondered why he had come. Did he just come back to comfort her? Did he need to see her again?

In another case, a young girl, only ten years old at the time, saw the ghost of a young man who had been engaged to marry one of the

Ghostly spirits appear near their headstones in the Anglican church cemetery in St. Thomas.

members of her church. She was terrified when he appeared before her and said she would never forget those seeking eyes. Too frightened to comprehend the situation, she ran and hid herself in a closet. This, however, proved to be no barrier for the ghost, who promptly joined her. She burst from the closet and ran. She never saw him again.

One Friday in 1967, a young man and his cousin left together on a weekend trip. The next morning the young man's mother heard footsteps pounding up the stairs and then came to a stop. She said to her husband, "That's our son, I wonder why he's come home." The boys were not due back until the next day.

She jumped out of bed to investigate, but no one was in the hall and there was no sign of her son in his room. Somewhat upset, she returned to bed.

On the Sunday they received word that their son and their nephew had drowned, but the bodies had not yet been found. The mother owned a grandfather clock, which had belonged to her first husband. It had never kept time since it had been moved to the house, but when her husband had died it bonged just once, in the middle of the night, and then returned to silence. Her son had been working on the clock the week before he went on his camping trip.

On the following Wednesday, the mother was dusting the clock and noticed that the key was missing. It had always been kept in the same place. That same evening, while sitting in the living room, she heard the cat clawing on the hardwood floor by the clock.

"Whatever is that cat up to?" she remarked to her husband. Later that same evening, on their way to bed, they saw the cat jump sideways when he walked past the clock. The next day the key to the clock was back in its proper place.

This happened three times in three days, and on the fourth day the son's body was found.

What was the mysterious connection to the clock?

SAVING LIVES ON THE FRENCH RIVER

Was it fate? I still sit and wonder in the safety of my home. Had we learned a lesson during that hour of discovery? The paddles now hang above the stone hearth. The haunting image of life and death is a question mark, etched in the grain of the wood.

So often, when one discovers Ontario, one discovers themselves. For myself and seven other men, death travelled swiftly in the current of all things one weekend, and life resembled the storm that crossed the waters. Nature encompassed us all.

It was a stormy afternoon when the men set their canoes in the dark waters of Wolsley Bay on the French River. The sky resembled the eerie depths of the channel. Facing sixty-kilometre winds, the men turned the point and headed their canoes down the river.

Losing control of my canoe, I caught my own image reflected in the water. Regaining my balance, I headed for shore where I was rescued by my Aboriginal friend, Two Bears. Minutes passed, and once again we headed out together in one canoe, towing mine behind. Two other men, Brian and Brent, held back, concerned about our safety. The four of us continued on, attempting to remain in harmony with the elements. The wind continued to increase.

We stopped halfway to our destination, to light a fire, warm our hands, and dry our clothes. Four hours later we reached our base camp at Starvation Bay, next to the Cedar Rapids.

Early morning on the French River.

The other four men had arrived earlier and had set up camp, with a raging fire burning.

Camped on bald rock that was dotted with gnarled pine overlooking the French River, we rested and we appreciated the landscape. As I gazed at my surroundings, I could see the history of these waters: the unchanged, still wilderness; the fur traders cutting a sharp edge, slicing the middle of the river with the strokes of their paddles; the cries of a loon; and the haunting howl of a wolf at night.

The French River, an hour north of Parry Sound, remains very much as it was first discovered — a timeless place where one can truly experience the past.

Having survived the trip down river and nestled from the wind in the safety of a cove we rested for the night. The wind still howled, the next day white caps appeared on the river. The day passed quietly. Two Bears, Michael, and I decided to fish along the cove at dusk.

At about 9:15 p.m. we started to paddle back to camp. We met a motor boat carrying two men. A light in the dark had saved their lives. This father and son had gone fishing that day, but lost their bearings.

They were travelling the river at night with no running lights, no map, compass, only one paddle, and very low on gas. They had continued to search for help.

The light they saw was a flashlight at our base camp. If they had not seen the light, they would have turned left, travelled down the rapids, and quite possibly have drowned. If we had not been there, one wonders the tragedy that would have followed.

Call it an act of fate or call it a miracle!

Starvation Bay and base camp on the French River.

THE ROSWELL CRASH

It was July 2, 1947. Mr. and Mrs. Dan Witmot were sitting on their front porch when what appeared to be a flying saucer passed over Roswell, New Mexico. It was heading northwest at a tremendous speed.

On Thursday, July 3, Frank Kaufmann, a military radar expert, at White Sands, New Mexico, tracked a mysterious object as it flashed through the atmosphere. This continued for the next twenty-four hours.

On Friday, July 4, William Woody and his father observed a bright light forty miles north of Roswell. The object had a flame-like tail and streaked across the night sky before disappearing beyond the horizon. At 11:27 p.m., on that same day, military personnel, who had been tracking the object for three days, saw it pulsate repeatedly on their screen and then explode. At exactly the same time, William Brazel, operator of the J.B. Foster Ranch, observed the worst lightning storm he had ever seen. Brazel also heard an explosion. At precisely that time, Jim Ragsdale and Trudy Truelove, who were camping in the New Mexico desert approximately forty miles northwest of Roswell, also saw a flowing bright light that passed over their heads and crashed within a mile of their campsite.

They jumped into their jeep and went in search of the downed craft. At the edge of a cliff they saw a craft embedded into the side of a slope. They decided to wait until morning to investigate.

On July 5, William Brazel rode his horse across some pasture land where he discovered a large quantity of strange debris scattered over an area about half a kilometre long and several hundred metres wide.

Kal Korff, in his book entitled, *The Roswell UFO Crash*, described the debris. "The material was highly unusual in nature and consisted mostly of tinfoil-type metal, only darker. The strange thing about the metal was that you could wrinkle it and lay it back down and it immediately resumed its original shape.

"Brazel noticed that on some of the debris there were mysterious markings or figures. He later described them as being comparable to New Mexico Indian petroglyphs."

Meanwhile, Jim Ragsdale and Trudy Truelove woke up at sunrise and immediately drove to the crash site. Korff added, "For the first time the couple got a clear look at the strange craft. They noticed loose debris scattered everywhere. Ragsdale later stated 'You could take that stuff and wad it up and it would straighten itself out.'"

The couple encountered an even more astounding sight. Ragsdale said, "There were bodies or something lying there. They looked like bodies."

The United States military soon arrived at the location of the downed spacecraft. An elite military team recovered the craft and the alien bodies at the site.

Ragsdale and Truelove observed the military arrive and quickly fled the site, undetected.

According to Korff, "Dan Dwyer and his fellow firemen from the Roswell Fire Department arrived at the site. Dwyer observed two body bags being loaded into one vehicle."

The corpses were taken back to the Roswell Army Air Field base.

The U.S. military had, by then, completely secured the area and had begun a massive clean-up. After a total of six hours, no trace of the crash remained.

At approximately 1:30 p.m. on July 5, Glenn Dennis, with the Ballard Funeral Home in Roswell, received a call from the base mortuary officer at the Roswell Army Air Field. The officer inquired about caskets — how small were the caskets that could be hermetically sealed?

Korff stated, "The Ballard Funeral Home had a contract with the Roswell Army Air Field at the time to handle the mortuary and other funeral-related affairs. Dennis was curious and offered to help out. The mortuary officer from the Air Field base declined his offer."

The International UFO Museum and Research Center. Roswell, New Mexico.

Signs were posted to keep the public away from the Roswell site.

Later that night Dennis was involved in driving an injured airman to the base infirmary. The infirmary and mortuary were in the same building. Dennis saw Naomi Maria Self, a nurse and friend of his at the infirmary. A colonel caught sight of Dennis and had two military police escort him off base and all the way back to the Ballard Funeral Home.

The following day Maria invited Dennis to meet her at the officers' club for lunch. Maria appeared to be in shock and a bit frightened. She told Dennis that there were three alien bodies. They were all dead and two of them were badly mutilated.

Sergeant Melvin Brown, a guard at the impact site, later described the aliens.

Korff stated, "Peering under the tarp, Brown saw the bodies of the alien flight crew and described them as small (in size), with large heads and skin that appeared yellow or orange.

"The alien corpses were flown out in a series of secret flights, first to Andrews Air Force base, and later to Wright-Paterson Air Force base in Ohio. The reason for the stop at Andrews was so that the army chief of staff and future president of the United States, Dwight Eisenhower, could view them. The alien bodies were eventually taken to Washington, D.C."

During the incident of the flying saucer, Lieutenant Walter Haut was instructed by Colonel Blanchard to draft a press release for radio stations and newspapers in Roswell. "The many rumours regarding the flying disc became a reality yesterday, when the Roswell Army Air Field was fortunate enough to gain possession of a disc. The flying object landed on a ranch near Roswell sometime last week."

The press release was on radio stations throughout the world.

Shortly thereafter, Colonel Blanchard received a call from Brigadier-General Roger Ramey, who expressed his extreme displeasure

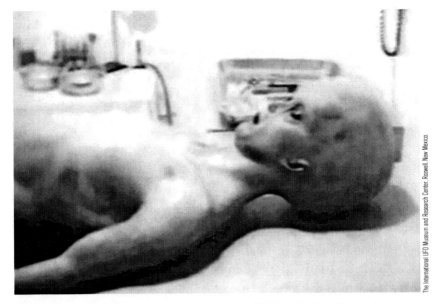

The autopsy of a Roswell alien from footage released in 1990. The film, *Alien Autopsy*, has been discredited as a hoax.

over the fact that a press release had been issued without proper author-ity. Colonel Blanchard went on leave.

General Ramey then announced "that the whole flying saucer affair was a mistake and that the debris recovered … was nothing more than the remains of a weather balloon."

The cover-up had begun. All witnesses to the crash site were threat-ened or sworn to secrecy. There was never any mention of the recovery of aliens. Nonetheless, Korff mentioned several times in his book that one alien had been found alive and unharmed at the site.

According to Randle and Schmitt in their book entitled *The Truth about the Roswell Crash*, Major Edwin Easley, who had been provost marshal in charge of the military police at the Roswell Army Air Field confirmed to Randle that there were indeed alien bodies. Randle wrote, "On his deathbed Easley was reluctant to talk of bodies, but finally, before he died, he said that he had seen them. He had been close enough to them to know they weren't human. He called them creatures."

Korff also highlighted a comment made by the Roswell fireman Dan Dwyer who had been at the crash site. "Dwyer observed a live alien."

Korff cited a letter that had been received by Art Bell, host of "Coast to Coast," on April 8, 1996. The letter had been signed, "a friend." "I would like to briefly tell you what my own grandfather told me about Roswell.

"My granddad stated the team arrived at the crash site just after the Air Force reported the ground zero location. They found two dead occupants hurled free of the disc. A lone surviving occupant was found within the disc and it was apparent its left leg was broken.

"Granddad was part of the team that went with the surviving occu-pant. The occupant communicated via telepathic means. The disc was a probe ship dispatched from a launch ship that was stationed at the dimensional gateway to the Terran Solar System, thirty-two light years from Terra."

This intriguing story also has a Canadian connection, to Wilbert Brockhouse Smith, the director of ionospheric measurement stations across Canada in 1953. He was also director of Project Magnet, a top-secret operation investigating flying saucers and the theory that their mode of propulsion utilized the magnetic fields of the earth and solar system.

Wilbert Smith had been working intimately with the highest offices of Canadian and American military intelligence and with the White House in the early 1950s.

It is documented that Smith had been given access to the alien bodies and to the Roswell flying saucer.

When asked about the existence of aliens, Smith stated, "It is my opinion that the people from the outside are so much like us that they could mingle with us and we would be none the wiser."

What do you think?

PROJECT MAGNET

On December 2, 1950, the Canadian government launched a top-secret mission to collect data on UFOs and to apply any recovered data to practical engineering and future technology.

The main government goal was the application of any findings on the subject of geomagnetism in order to use the Earth's magnetic field as a source of propulsion for vehicles. The project, entitled "Project Magnet" was under the direction of Wilbert B. Smith, senior radio engineer for the Department of Transport.

Wilbert Smith's direct involvement in UFO research had begun in September 1950, while he was attending a conference in Washington, D.C. He had just read Frank Scully's recently published book, *Behind the Flying Saucer*. The book had referred to flying saucer crashes in New Mexico and to their ability to utilize magnetic principals in their propulsion. This information had drawn Smith's attention.

On September 15, 1950, a military attaché, Lieutenant Colonel Bremner, arranged a meeting with Dr. Robert Sarbacher, an electrical engineer and guided-missile scientist who told Smith that flying saucers did exist and did not originate on Earth.

The subject of flying saucers according to Dr. Sarbacher, at that time, was the most highly classified subject in the United States' government, and at a higher level than even the H-bomb.

Project Magnet started out small, using the Department of Transport facilities and other departments, including the Defense Research Board and the National Research Council.

On April 22, 1952, the Defence Research Board directed staff member Harold Oatway to form a committee to study flying saucer reports. The committee gathered together and classified their work as confidential and identified themselves as Project Theta. Smith was involved with this group as well. On May 19, 1952, the group met again and renamed themselves Project Second Story, since *Theta* was apparently not on the list of valid names for projects of this type.

In October 1953, Smith established the first flying saucer sighting station at Shirley's Bay, outside of Ottawa. The station consisted of a small wooden Defence Research Board building containing highly sophisticated instrumentation specifically adapted for the detection of flying saucers. The instruments were a gamma-ray counter, a magnetometer, a radio receiver, and a recording gravimeter. These four instruments produced traces on a multiple-pen graphical recorder, which was checked periodically to note any disturbances.

During June 1953, Smith submitted an interim report. He stated in his report that it appeared evident that flying saucers are emissaries from some other civilization and actually do operate on magnetic principals. During an interview he revealed that he had been loaned, by a very high level United States agency that he wouldn't name, a piece of metal for analysis. The metal object had allegedly come from a small flying saucer during flights over Washington.

That same year the Canadian government acknowledged a notable increase in the number of UFO incidents covered by the Canadian newspaper organizations. In particular, there were reports of disc-shaped craft over Canadian Air Force bases.

At 3:01 p.m. on August 8, 1954, something believed to be a flying saucer flew over the Shirley's Bay UFO station. The staff of Project Magnet were being observed!

The instrumentation at the station registered a definite disturbance, quite different from disturbances registered by passing aircraft. Smith and his colleagues were alerted by a built-in alarm system. Staff rushed outside only to find a heavy overcast sky. The spacecraft was hidden in the clouds. Their only evidence was a very large and unexplainable deflection registered on the chart recorder paper.

The Canadian government was forced to acknowledge Project Magnet. The media had discovered this covert government mission. A press release went out on August 10, 1954, revealing that the Department of Transport had been engaged in the study of UFOs for the past three and a half years. The facility was required to close down. Smith, however, was allowed to continue his research in his own free time. He was still allowed to use government equipment, not otherwise in use, and the Shirley's Bay facilities. He did so until his death in 1962.

On June 11, 1959, Wilbert Smith gave a lecture to the Illuminating Engineering Society, in Ottawa, highlighting his research. This is what he had to say.

> During the past ten years I have made a serious and extensive study of the phenomena of flying saucers. I have covered every aspect that I could come to grips with, and have arrived at some conclusions. I think that many of these objects are spacecraft, and that they come from elsewhere than on this planet, that they are built and operated by beings much like us, but who are more advanced in the business of living than we are, and that the saucers represent a technology which is much ahead of ours.
>
> I have interviewed many people who claimed to have seen a flying saucer, and I am convinced they are normal, honest folk who are reporting, as best they can, something which they actually did witness.
>
> We have in addition to visual evidence a variety of confirmations in other forms. Physical evidence of witnessed landings, such as imprints in soft ground, broken bushes, withered vegetation, etc. Various items of "hardware" are known to exist, but are usually promptly clapped into security and therefore are not available to the general public. Substances such as "angel hair" and molten tin, etc., have been observed to drop from these craft.

I think that there is too much evidence to ignore that the saucers are real and extraterrestrial spacecraft, and since their behaviours cannot adequately be explained by our science, we are forced to the conclusion that this alien science transcends ours, and may even be beyond our reach.

THE ABORIGINAL HAUNTING IN ORILLIA

Mrs. Johnston of Bowmanville, Ontario, wrote to tell me of an unusual occurrence in Orillia. This story took place in the 1930s when she and her brother were young teenagers.

Our parents bought a lot on the outskirts of Orillia, one that seemed to never been used in any way.

The property was situated on a large hill that overlooked a lake. The hillside was dotted with many boulders. The house they built was a hip-roof style and had a dormer window upstairs with a fine view of the Lake Couchiching.

One evening in the summer at sunset my mother started upstairs, stopped on the landing, which had a dormer window, turned to go up the few steps to the hall, and saw there, at the end of the hall, standing in the opposite dormer window, an Aboriginal person, wearing the full head-dress of a chief. She stayed perfectly still and a few moments later he faded from view.

This happened several times over the next five years, always in late evening. Then my mother had part of the hip roof, beside the dormer window, closed in to make a cupboard. That was the end of the apparition.

In working the garden around the house we unearthed many stone arrowheads, which knowledgeable people said were such as the Aboriginal people used and we wondered if this spot had been used by them.

Apparently Orillia was once the site of an Aboriginal village before 1840. I have enjoyed your program over the years and feel we are very fortunate to have you to keep alive some of the down-to-earth history of our province.

My research supports her story. The town of Orillia, situated at the narrows between Lake Simcoe and Lake Couchiching, enjoys an advantageous location on both Highway 11 and Highway 12, and on the Trent Canal system. The first recorded white man to set foot on site of the present-day Orillia was Samuel de Champlain. He spent the winter of 1615 at a fortified Huron village situated at the narrows near the site of the present city of Orillia.

As late as 1850, the township was still sparsely settled. Much of the land was reserved for the Aboriginal peoples in accordance with treaties made in the 1820s. The village of Orillia had been selected as an Aboriginal post, which became the headquarters for the Chippewa tribe. It was here that a house was built for Chief Yellowhead. The presence of the Aboriginal population slowed down the settlement of newly arrived immigrants. The Chippewas were not anxious for settlers to locate in their immediate vicinity. However, in 1839, responding to a petition by the settlers, the Chippewas were moved to Rama Township and a survey was made of their former lands.

One group of Aboriginal people participated in an assimilation experiment at Coldwater, Ontario, near Lake Simcoe. A group of Ojibwa were gathered together on the Coldwater reserve to be instructed in agricultural arts, but the experiment was a failure. Among the contributing factors was a general lack of understanding of Aboriginal culture, needs, and values. The Ojibwa fishermen and hunters regarded agricultural work as demeaning and were unable to appreciate the value of jobs such as road building, which was non-essential in the context of their culture.

In regards to the Johnston home there is another piece of history. Approximately three hundred years ago, the Ojibwa fought numerous battles with the Iroquois who were positioned in the central and southern parts of Ontario, including Orillia. A battle between the Iroquois and Ojibwa is recorded as taking place on or near the very hill of the Johnston home. One wonders how old some of our apparitions might be.

FAIRIES AND THE ELEMENTAL WORLD

The fairy realm exists in the otherworld where linear, measurable time does not exist. It is a place with a host of elementals of all shapes, sizes, and characteristics.

The word elemental is used to describe the "little people," including leprechauns, elves, goblins, gnomes, trolls, sprites, fairies, brownies — just some of the words used to name them. People around the world have encountered elementals throughout the ages. Although encounters today maybe less frequent, they are possible. These magical experiences alter your life forever.

Gossamer Penwyche (a pen name) is such a person who once encountered the otherworld.

"I believe in fairies. My belief is based on a simple, childlike experience I have never forgotten. I was in the woods that bordered the property of my childhood home. I was alone and unafraid playing in one of my favourite haunts, a stream that lay in a hollow of one of the numerous waterfalls that can be found along the Bruce Trail in Southern Ontario."

The time was midday and midsummer. According to Gossamer in her book, *The World of Fairies*, gateways to the otherworld can be accessed by mortals at times and places that are in between — neither here nor there, then nor now. Dusk, dawn, midnight, and midday are all times that lie between darkness and light, night and day, morning and afternoon, and are reputedly the most auspicious times for seeking out fairies.

The sun was high in the sky as Gossamer played by herself. Suddenly, a gust of wind threatened to topple her off the rock on which she stood in the middle of the stream. She sat down quickly on a broad flat rock that protruded several centimetres above water. A sudden, sharp cry announced the arrival of a hawk. The bird had landed on one of the lowest branches of an ancient oak rooted near the stream. The massive branches created a magical canopy overhead.

Gossamer added, "A faint breeze started up again, whirling around me in circles, warm and embracing. I felt as if I were at the vortex of a small tornado and began to sway in spiralling, synchronized motion with the wind."

The songbirds that had ceased singing with the arrival of the hawk, began again to sing. Then Gossamer heard something else.

"Rising above the melodious 'song of birds,' I could discern the sound of sweet, youthful voices singing a lighthearted tune."

Then the song ended and the hawk let out another cry. The hawk stretched its wings and took off suddenly, flying directly towards Gossamer. She explained, "I threw my hands up to protect myself. It came so close that I could feel the rush of its wings on my cheeks as it flew by me. My fear turned to amazement when I caught a glimpse of the hawk's large, fan-shaped tail. It looked like a feathered cape or the train of a doll's dress. I was so startled that I slipped off the rock and fell into the stream. I was certain that I heard children's laughter as I struggled to sit upright, waist-high in water. I looked all around me for the source of the laughter but saw no one."

Something else had occurred that left her speechless and wanting. "When I finally came back to my ordinary senses I noticed that the sun was no longer in its usual noon-day position, but was resting quite low in the western sky. Several hours had lapsed while I had noticed only a few minutes."

Gossamer, instead of feeling puzzled by this loss of time, felt only disappointment.

"I wanted to be in that weird and wondrous place I had been in just moments before. I wanted the magic to return. My fairy encounter, for I have no doubt that is what it was, has haunted me all my life."

Tanis Helliwell is an organizational consultant and teacher of inner mysteries. She teaches spiritual development and leads tours to the Earth's sacred sites. In 1997 she authored *Summer with the Leprechauns*, a true story about an encounter with the elemental world in Ireland.

While in Ireland living in an old thatched-roof cottage, Tanis encountered a family of leprechauns. These seldom-seen beings taught her about the evolution of elementals — that race to which leprechauns, elves, goblins, gnomes, trolls, fairies, and devas belong. This is her story.

"After a half-hour walk, I came to a small, white cottage, with a slate roof and a blue door, surrounded by a white fence.

"Since entering, I had felt as if I was intruding on someone's home. I was convinced that I was being watched. My eyes swung over to the corner from which these vibrations emanated. I was shocked to find four people watching me: a small man, a small woman, and two children. I thought, but what strange clothes they're wearing. My God, they're human."

According to Tanis, the family of leprechauns spoke to her. "We've lived in this cottage for a hundred of your years and we're willing to share it with you."

Tanis described their appearance. "He was no more than four feet tall and was dressed in an old-fashioned buttoned-up green jacket that ended at his waist. Brown trousers, cut off at the knee, extended down to thick leggings, which were inserted into large clog shoes and completing his strange attire was a gigantic black top hat.

"The two boys were miniature versions of their father, minus the protruding stomach and top hat. The little woman was dressed in a full skirt down to the floor and the same style clogs of her husband. She had on a hat that reminded me of those worn by the New England pilgrims, which seemed too large for her head."

The elder leprechaun warned Tanis that she was living on a haunted lane where not all the elementals were friendly to humans. He told her she would need their protection if she intended to live the summer there.

The leprechaun then stated, "We elementals have got this theory that maybe humans have made themselves coarse and dense on purpose, so that they can't see us and other beings. They are too consumed in themselves."

Her experience that summer opened a new door in her life and changed her forever. I could regale you with endless stories about that world but perhaps you need to seek out your own "otherworld" experience instead. Spend more time by streams and water with your heart and ears open and your mind at rest.

A PIONEER OF
PARANORMAL RESEARCH

During the early 1930s people were gathering around tables and holding séances. The paranormal was of interest to many Canadians. In fact, the interest peaked shortly after the First World War, when relatives attempted to communicate with their deceased sons and daughters.

Dr. Hamilton of Winnipeg could be considered to be the pioneer of paranormal research in Canada. From 1918 to the mid-1930s, Hamilton discovered whether or not communication between the living and the deceased was possible.

For nearly two decades, a veritable smorgasbord of paranormal investigation and activity took place in the Hamilton home. It was during this same period that spiritualism flourished in Canada and elsewhere. Guests would gather in the parlour of someone's home and participate in séances.

According to author Barbara Smith in her book *Ghost Stories of Manitoba*, "Those attending the Hamilton séances were introduced to 'table-tipping,' a paranormal activity that at the time was considered to be little more than a parlour game."

To communicate with spirits people would sit in a circle and place their hands on a table. Then the group would attempt to make contact with the spirit world. According to Smith, "In response to a system pre-determined by the people attending, spirits would lift the table a few centimetres off the floor, angle slightly and, with one or two legs, tap or knock on the floor. One knock would usually represent a positive answer, two a negative reply."

Eventually this led to a more sophisticated system with one tap standing for the letter A and two for the letter B, and so on.

Few Canadians knew, at the time, that their own prime minister, William Lyon Mackenzie King, communicated regularly with his dead dog and with certain biblical characters. Dr. Hamilton once facilitated such a visitation for Prime Minister Mackenzie King when he was alive.

The doctor had a strong background in medicine and research and attempted to pursue the paranormal in a scientific fashion. The method he employed was photography. His photographic efforts captured images of spirits that had been called forth by the participants in his home.

Hundreds of photographs that were taken during the Hamilton séances are now housed in the archival collections at the University of Manitoba.

In a book called *Intention and Survival*, published in 1930, Dr. Hamilton outlined some of his methods. This body of work featured a séance demonstration done with strictly controlled procedures in order to eliminate any misconceptions. Isaac Pitblada was a respected lawyer who was the uninvolved observer of the experiment.

During the séance, a spirit by the name of Walter made his presence known. A designated photographer in the group shot a series of photographs during the communication with the spirit. The spirit, Walter, was captured on photographic plates. The success of this séance encouraged the group to continue their communications with the deceased using cameras to verify the existence of such spirits.

By the mid-1930s North America was experiencing a severe depression. The fascination with spiritualism quickly disappeared from the landscape.

Dr. Hamilton died in the spring of 1935. Those close to the doctor continued his paranormal work for a time. In 1938, Dr. Hamilton communicated with his old friends during a séance. He assured a former associate that he was fine and was accompanied by author Sir Arthur Conan Doyle, who also had had a great interest in the world of spiritualism. The two men had known and respected one another in life.

Recently, psychic Shelley O'Day visited the Hamilton house and confirmed the presence of a spirit. It would seem the other spirits who once visited the home are just waiting for an invitation to return.

In his book *History of Ghosts*, Peter H. Aykroyd tells another tale of his great-grandfather, Dr. Samuel Augustus, who presided over his own home circle, featuring sitters and a medium. This took place in the Aykroyd house in Sydenham, Ontario.

Actor Dan Aykroyd, Peter's brother, adds, "Part of *Ghostbusters* the movie originated from my great-grandfathers interest in spiritualism and from the books he collected. He bequeathed these to his son, my grandfather, Maurice. His son, my father, as a child witnessed séances and kept the family books on the subject. My brother Peter and I read them avidly and became lifelong supporters of the American Society for Psychical Research, and from all this *Ghostbusters* got made."

The prologue describes the setting prior to a séance at the Aykroyd home on May 12, 1929.

Four cars, all black, roll down the long lane to the farmhouse. The occupants alight. Four men in three-piece suits with well-shined shoes form a little knot. The women, four of them as well, all in black with stylish hats, form a companion group.

Grandpa has invited the guests to be seated. The drapes are drawn. As the guests file into the parlour, they nod significantly to the seated young man and take their places.

The young man leans back, closes his eyes, and slips into a trance.

This is a meeting of Dr. Aykroyd's circle. A séance is about to begin. The people have come from town to talk to the dead.

THE GHOST ROAD

Over the years hundreds of people have travelled to Scugog Island's Ghost Road, near the small community of Port Perry, to see a mysterious light that haunts the somewhat deserted side road. Many believe the spirit of a headless motorcyclist still appears on this lonely stretch of road near the shores of Lake Scugog.

Sometime during the late sixties, according to local lore, a terrible accident took place on this road, which runs north-south between the Ninth and Tenth Concessions. Since the road is seldom travelled many romantically inclined young people find it a convenient place to park. A long stretch of road such as this tends to appeal to anyone with a yen for speed. As the story goes, a young motorcyclist from out of town chose to test his speed here one night. Travelling southbound and much too fast, he suddenly caught sight of the end of the road, the Ninth Concession. Approximately one hundred metres from the south end, near a large old willow tree, he lost control and barrelled off into a corn field where he struck a rusty wire fence and was decapitated.

In 1984, Matt Grant, a Port Perry High School student, parked on Ghost Road with his girlfriend and two other couples. The boys all thought it would be a great idea to scare the girls with the story of the decapitated ghost rider. Matt got more than he bargained for when he had the most frightening experience of his life.

They were in the only car parked on the Ghost Road. For one hour they sat, waiting for the light to appear. Suddenly dashboard lights lit

The Ghost Road, where a sphere of light appears at night, near the spot where a motorcyclist was reported to have died.

up and the radio began to turn on and off. Everyone in the car started screaming, especially when the door locks began to move up and down on their own as well. Matt later said, "The crazy part of this was that I didn't know what to do. You see, the keys to the car were in my pocket. I couldn't believe this was happening to us. Then the headrest started rocking me back and forth in my seat. Then it ended." To add to their fear, Matt said that wolves were howling during their ordeal.

Some skeptics are convinced the ghost light is just a case of car headlights, travelling down the hilly West Quarter Line, which runs almost directly in the same north-south line as the Ghost Road, a few kilometres across the lake. When a vehicle travels down the West Quarter Line, at an elevation of more than a three hundred metres, it appears on the lower Ghost Road as a single light coming out of the darkness near the tree line, slowly moving downward and seeming closer than it really is.

In July 1983, Cathy Robb, a journalist with the *Port Perry Star*, began an investigation into the Ghost Road story. Ms. Robb contacted a retired

Ontario Provincial Police officer, Harold Hockins, who had patrolled the island for many years. Mr. Hockins told Ms. Robb, "I've policed the island since 1954 and I've never heard tell of any fatal accident involving a motorcycle."

The next month, a ghost-hunting team gathered at the newspaper office in Port Perry armed with walkie-talkies, CB radios, a camera with infra-red film, two cameras with regular film, a high-powered flashlight, and three vehicles. Part of the group had walkie-talkies and set up on the Ghost Road. The other members of the group drove up and down the West Quarter Line. Their headlights soon appeared on the Ghost Road as one light floating out of the night sky. Then they stopped, turned off the headlights, and figured they'd put the phantom out of business.

Then the radio started chattering, "Okay, we see your lights," said a voice on the Ghost Road.

"We don't have our lights on," replied the group on the West Quarter Line.

"Well, we see the light."

In 1986, six Niagara College film students showed up to do a short documentary and capture the ghost light on film. On the first evening everyone prepared for the arrival of the floating light. One student, stationed in the field at the south end of the road where the rider supposedly hit the fence, claims a sphere of light the size of a basketball popped out of thin air and hovered about twenty metres away for a few seconds.

The students not only managed to photograph the light, but video tape it as well. When the photograph was developed it revealed the fuzzy outline of a human figure bathed in a strong white light — an aura. On the video tape the figure is more defined and appears to have legs.

Have you any interest in the mysterious lights on Ghost Road?

Perhaps the next time you find yourself travelling east on Highway 7a out of Port Perry, sometime after dusk, you will head left up Scugog Island and test your own ability to see the lights on the infamous Ghost Road.

ALIEN ENCOUNTER IN ONTARIO

On Tuesday evening, October 7, 1975, an alien spacecraft appeared in the night sky over Muskoka. It landed twenty-one kilometres northwest of Bracebridge, in the Raymond Valley near Three Mile Lake. What seemed to be an impossibility to some residents of the valley quickly became a terrifying and fearful nightmare for others.

Shirley Greer and her brother, Robert Suffern, thought they had just stepped into the Twilight Zone. For a short time they felt they were beyond reality, a place where uncertainty and fear gripped their very souls.

It all began for them at 8:00 p.m., when Shirley sighted what she described as a glow in the sky down a dirt road adjacent to her brother's place. It looked to her as though the barn there was on fire. She phoned her brother to tell him what she had seen. He thanked her but assured her his barn was not on fire.

Shirley later shared with Jamie Lamb, a journalist with the *Packet and Times* newspaper in Muskoka, what happened next. "I decided to go down to my brother's house and babysit the children while Robert went to investigate the glow. Mrs. Suffern was away at the time."

Shirley had watched this glow die away in the sky, but in a most peculiar way. "You know, the way a fire dies with the light fading the furthest points in the sky and then the light recedes down to the source. This glow faded upwards into nothing."

Robert left the house, got in his car, and headed west in search of the glow. He drove down a hill half a kilometre from his place, where a row of cottages stood by Three Mile Lake. Then he saw it! Lamb added, "Illuminated in the high-beam headlights some 150 feet ahead of the car there was a spacecraft."

Robert said, "It was about twelve to fourteen feet across and about eight or nine feet high. There was a black stripe running around its circumference and there was what looked to be a small landing platform at the bottom of the vehicle. There were no lights, markings, or antenna on the spacecraft."

Jamie Lamb added, "Mr. Suffern said there was no dust raised, no apparent thrust, nothing. It just went up and away."

Robert had seen enough. He had no idea he was about to encounter one of the occupants of the craft.

Still shaken from his experience, he turned the car around and headed back up the road to his home. As he crested the hill, his headlights picked something else up. There in the middle of the road stood a three-foot creature dressed all in silver. Robert swerved to avoid hitting the alien and then slammed on his brakes.

"He, or it, was just a little higher than the front fender of the car. He was dressed completely in silver but his helmet was a little lighter than his suit. The suit looked like tinfoil that was crushed and then flattened," stated Robert.

Jamie Lamb added, "He said the creature had two arms, two legs, a glove-shaped helmet, and walked similarly to a midget."

Robert explained to Jamie what happened next. "It turned, pivoted, actually, took four or five steps, and then vaulted over the fence. I'll never forget it going over the fence. It put both hands on the fence post and all in one regular motion vaulted over the fence effortlessly, like he had no weight."

Mrs. Greer later reported that when the spacecraft was hovering outside the house, the television set lost its picture and sound. "Just went static," she recalled.

Carol Suffern, Robert's wife, returned shortly after the event. She became alarmed when she saw how scared her husband was. The couple decided to report their encounter to the Ontario Provincial Police, who arrived and conducted an investigation. The *Packet and Times* reported that the police found no reason to doubt Mr. Suffern's sighting.

The family had no idea of the media attention this story would attract. The Sufferns, whether they liked it or not, had been impacted by the event. They eventually sold and left Muskoka.

One wonders what the aliens were doing in the Raymond Valley. Were they looking for something, or was it just a stopover? This has not been the only UFO sighting in Muskoka. Maybe there's a tourist attraction for alien tourists too.

THE MOUND BUILDERS

Monuments of past civilizations lie scattered in many parts of the world. Egypt has her pyramids and England has her Stonehenge. The stone cities of the Mayans adorn Mexico's Yucatán Peninsula. In the continent of North America, we have very few spectacular relics of prehistory.

To view the signs of our past we must look, not just to the vast monuments of imperishable stone, but to subtler things: the arrowhead in the forest soil, the image carved on the face of a cliff, the piece of broken pottery. Men in search of myths will find those things.

In Mexico and in South and Central America, European invaders found past kingdoms and awesome overgrown cities, but the land to the north seemed to be a continent of woods and plains, inhabited by simple huntsmen and equally simple farmers. It seemed to offer no stirring symbols of vanished greatness. Was there nothing to compare to the treasures of the Old World? The answer was yes, there was.

As colonists gradually spread westward and southward, they found strange earthen mounds beyond the Alleghenies and in the valley of the Mississippi. The mounds seemed to lack in beauty and elegance. They were incredibly rounded heaps of earth. Some were colossal, like one mound in Illinois that was thirty metres high and covered sixteen acres. Not only that, the numbers were also incredible — ten thousand in the Ohio River Valley alone. Most of them contained human bones, weapons, tools, and jewellery.

In the north, the mound zone began in western New York and extended along the southern shore of Lake Erie into what are now

Michigan and Wisconsin, and on to Iowa and Nebraska. In the south, mounds lined the Gulf of Mexico from Florida to eastern Texas; on up through the Carolinas and across to Oklahoma.

By the early nineteenth century, hundreds (if not thousands) of mounds had been examined, measured, and partially excavated. Many were destroyed by farming.

Along the Great Lakes, the mounds tended to be low — no more than a metre high — and took the forms of gigantic birds, reptiles, beasts, and men.

Isolated mounds in the form of immense, flat-topped pyramids were sometimes found in the Midwest. Some were terraced or had graded roadways to their summits. To their discoverers, it appeared probable that the flat-topped mounds had once been platforms for temples long ago destroyed by the elements. Their presence in the United States bordering the Gulf of Mexico clearly indicated some link between the Mayan culture and that of the builders of the mounds.

One theory of the mound builders was the migration of the Mayans from Mexico. When they arrived in what is now Florida, Georgia, and Louisiana, they built flat-topped temples of earth, similar to the stone temples in Mexico. As each generation moved northward, their ancestral culture faded and different forms of mounds were constructed. When they reached what is now Canada, the mounds became even smaller. Whatever the theory, they do exist.

A number of mounds exist on the north shore of Rice Lake in Ontario. They are called the Serpent Mounds.

We may never know the true meaning of the mounds, but what we can see certainly stirs ones imagination.

SERPENT MOUNDS

It was late August in 1896 when an archaeologist by the name of David Boyle ventured forth into the field for what was about to become the most thrilling four weeks of his archaeological experience.

Gerald Killan in his book *David Boyle*, described Boyle's adventures during this time. "To humour his friend H.T. Strickland of Peterborough, who was convinced of the existence of burial mounds on Rice Lake, a skeptical Boyle headed east to Peterborough County. The site in question was in Otonabee Township on the crest of a hill near the mouth of the Indian River on the north side of Rice Lake. As he plodded around the property which he noted had often been raided by relic hunters, Boyle observed four mounds and what appeared to be a zig-zag embankment nearly two hundred feet in length."

Boyle began excavation on the oval mound at the eastern extremity of the long earth structure. Killan adds, "He drove a trench five feet wide across the mound and made another cut from the western end to meet the first trench, the two thus forming a large T. His initial skepticism about the mounds soon dissipated upon finding, in the first opening, two skeletons in a sitting position, and a skull and long bones at a depth of two feet."

To Boyle, the discovery revealed recent burials. Another skeleton was found a metre below in the second trench. Near the centre of the mound, Boyle discovered burnt human bones and pottery fragments.

Killan described what Boyle did next. "For a wider perspective, he backed away from the structure to a ridge some fifty feet distant to the west. Suddenly it struck him — that end of the embankment was tapered. He scurried to the other extremity of the structure — it rose abruptly to a height of four feet. His mind raced and his thoughts turned to the Great Serpent Mound of Adams County, Ohio. Could this be an Ontario equivalent? He walked over and around the structure, observing if from every direction. Whatever his vantage point, he kept visualizing the head of a serpent at the eastern end of the mound."

Boyle observed a tapering tail to the west. The measurement of the structure confirmed that the zig-zag sections were twelve metres. He concluded that the structure was meant to be serpentine.

Killan added, "The position of the oval mound, accurately in line with the head and neck portion of the long structure, suggested the ancient combination of serpent and egg, just as in Adams County, Ohio."

Boyle later opened the four mounds lying along the south or lake-ward side of the serpent, and in every instance he found human remains.

He was adamant that this site be protected and preserved from relic hunters. He met with the owners of the property who agreed to sell the four-acre site for $450. The government, however, had no intention of creating a preserve. After all, they had only recently created Algonquin Park. They were not interested in the creation of another park, especially an Aboriginal burial ground.

Thankfully, the owners understood the significance of this discovery and guarded the property from vandals. In 1933, the Hiawatha band of the Mississauga nation purchased the property. In 1956, the First Nations leased the land to the Ontario Ministry of Natural Resources and Forestry to create a provincial park — sixty years after David Boyle first proposed the idea.

GHOSTS

Many people are convinced that they have seen a ghost. Do ghosts really exist? Unfortunately the evidence gathered is not always reliable. Many accounts of ghosts are so far-fetched that they are obviously nonsense or outright fakes. Other ghosts have been shown to be the result of odd light conditions playing tricks on the eyes. Some ghosts, however, do appear to be real.

Who believes in ghosts? In 1890, a survey was carried out in several European countries. Upwards of 17,000 people were questioned, and their answers provided some interesting insights in regards to ghosts. In that survey 1,684 people claimed to have seen a ghost.

In the seventeenth century, witch hunts were common and belief in the supernatural was common among people of every country. In southwest England, Reverend Dodge was quite a mad ghost hunter. He would run along roads with a whip, shouting and flogging unseen spirits. He also lurked in churchyards, waiting to trap ghosts. Whether he actually saw one has not been proven, but according to one story, one ghost he encountered was so frightened that it gave out a loud cry and vanished forever.

The Romans were careful to avoid ghosts. Special festivals were held every year in May to keep away evil spirits. Even today many people believe it is considered bad luck to be married in the month of May. During these festive celebrations, drums were often pounded for hours. The ghosts were supposed to be afraid of the noise and the din was thought to make them fly away in fright. Just to be sure, black beans were also burned by

It is possible to photograph ghosts. This female spirit was photographed in the Greystones Inn, Orangeville. One of the oldest buildings in the town, it is now a restaurant.

Author's Collection.

the sides of graves. The Romans believed that the foul-smelling smoke of the beans would be certain to keep ghosts away.

The people of the Banks Islands in the Pacific Ocean believed that certain stones were haunted by soul-hungry ghosts. If a person's shadow fell across such a stone the ghost was thought to suck out the person's soul. After losing their soul, they would die. These stones were placed in empty houses to keep away thieves.

In Mexico the ghosts of people who have died violently are said to be able to cure illness.

Japanese ghosts are believed to be deformed as a punishment for evil deeds when they were alive. Many are legless, their lower limbs engulfed in flames. According to legend, they warn people when death was near.

According to Rosemary Ellen Guiley in her book *The Encyclopedia of Ghosts and Spirits*, "Every culture had superstitions concerning ghosts. In European folklore, for example, it is widely believed that one should never touch a ghost; that ghosts cannot cross running water; that ghosts only appear at night; and that ghosts have noticeable smells. Smells are the second most common characteristic of a haunting."

Rosemary Guiley adds, "Frederic Myers did not believe that ghosts were conscious or intelligent entities, but rather believed they were automatic projections of consciousness which had their centres elsewhere. More recent researchers have disagreed, arguing that at least some ghosts may possess an awareness, perhaps within themselves."

It is widely believed in folklore throughout the world that persons born at a certain time of day, or on a particular day, possess the clairvoyant power to see ghosts and things that other persons cannot see. Guiley adds, "In Lancashire, England, children born during twilight are believed to have the ability to know which of their acquaintances will die next. In other parts of England, the magical birth hour is twelve o'clock at night or the hour after midnight.

"In parts of Europe, it is the day of birth that predicts the power to see clairvoyantly. In Scotland, people born on Christmas Day or Good Friday are said not only to be able to see spirits but to order them about."

John Carlos Perrone is a very intuitive, astute, and perceptive clairvoyant who I met years ago when researching the haunting of the Cawthra Estate in Mississauga, Ontario. At the time I needed to clarify who was still occupying the Cawthra Estate from the past. Was it Grace Cawthra, who was so adamant to remain, or Elizabeth, a servant, who called the estate home?

John was willing to meet with me and discuss my questions. He had recently toured the estate and had the information I needed to finish the story.

I met John in his office in Mississauga. He welcomed me with a firm handshake and pleasant smile. My first question was what is the difference between a clairvoyant and a psychic? He answered, "A psychic wants to be right. A good clairvoyant wants to be accurate, helpful, and healing.

"I once said to a woman I was reading that she had been married once. She immediately challenged me — I was wrong because she had been married three times. I replied that the only husband she had ever loved was the first one. It turned out that her other two marriages had only lasted two to three months. What I was saying was that she only had one real, loving marriage. She agreed."

I asked him when he first became aware of this gift to see the past and future.

He answered, "The earliest memory I have of awakening to this gift was age three or four. I recall being in the back seat of the car. We had just visited some friends of my parents. I looked at my mother and said it was too bad that her lady friend we had just seen was going to die next Wednesday. My family was horrified. Sure enough, the next Wednesday the woman was dead.

"My grandfather was a clairvoyant. He could communicate telepathically. He would be at his house and suddenly I would hear him tell me he was coming over and to put the coffee on. A few minutes later he would enter our house.

"My powers seem to be getting stronger as I get older. I now have spirits speak to me in other languages that I cannot understand. I can see them, but sometimes they are opaque, or orbs of light; or flashes of light; or shadows or energy imprints of people or events. For example, I can see the impression of the person who lived in a particular setting or even see a murder taking place."

I felt assured by now and asked specifically about the Cawthra Estate. What impressions had John picked up?

He responded, "My sense was, as I approached the house, that the focal point of spirit activity was in the attic.

"As I entered the house I knew there was no Grace Cawthra present. This very gracious woman has moved on. However, there are remnants of her energy still lingering. Her high intellectual energy knew to move on after her death.

"Yet people are constantly calling on her. These lookers and gogglers are calling on her energy to return. This drains her. She feels drawn from the other dimension. These people are harassing her. This is wrong.

"As I toured the house I immediately picked up male and female spirit energy. The male is the strongest."

John then shared his experiences as he entered the second floor and began to hike up the narrow staircase that led to the attic.

"As I approached the top of the stairs the male spirit told me to get out of there. Like a child, this male presence began stomping his feet. She yelled to her male companion to stop his antics.

"She was dressed in an ankle-length grey dress that bunched at the waist with puffy shoulders. She wore an apron over the dress that was somewhat soiled. She appeared to be in her mid-thirties. She is a kind woman who is happy to do her job. She died right here in the attic."

The description matched that of Elizabeth, Grace's loyal servant.

John added, "She doesn't like this male spirit energy in her space. This male is a relation who Grace had approached to inherit the estate. He is angry that I have identified him. He is getting really angry. He felt entitled to the property. He and Grace Cawthra had a disagreement concerning how she wanted things done. In his mind he knew he would outlive her. My feeling is he died before Grace and was unable to do the scheming he had envisioned.

"He is not a dangerous spirit, but a nasty person. He feels this is his house. He doesn't want anyone here.

"The female spirit still keeps the house in order. She loves the city employees who now work here. She also keeps the male spirit in line."

The question around the existence of ghosts or spirits will continue to challenge many of us. Clairvoyants may know the answer concerning the existence of sprits, but we may only know the answer after our own passing.

WHO MURDERED BILLY STONE?

Who really shot Bill Stone, the telegraph operator at Whitby Junction Station, on the snowy evening of December 11, 1914?

The twenty-one-year-old telegraph operator, William Stone Jr., would sit quietly at his desk in the Whitby Train Station, recording the trains that passed and noting any telegraph messages. This night seemed like any other. Nothing really exciting ever happened while the towns-people slept in their beds. Something was brewing that night, though. At 12:37 a.m. a shot was fired in the darkness. Billy Stone toppled from his chair and landed with a thud on the floor. By some miracle, he managed to crawl to the phone and call for help. Leslie Cormack, the operator for the local Bell telephone switchboard, answered his call.

"Get the chief, quick. I've been shot!" cried Billy Stone on the phone that fateful night.

"Who did it?" asked Cormack, while she dialed Police Chief Charles F. MacGrotty.

Stone answered, "I don't know, but get the chief quick."

When Chief MacGrotty picked up the phone, there was only silence. Was William dead?

The chief rushed downtown to fetch the night watchman, John Patterson. Together they travelled to the train station. It was an eerie sight. The shade on William's desk light had been turned to cast its rays of lights on the tracks. Peering in the window they saw Stone lying on the office floor. The telephone receiver was under his lifeless body.

The Whitby train station where Billy Stone was murdered on December 11, 1914. The building is now an art gallery called the Station Gallery.

They forced the door open and rushed to Stone. He was dead. The chief peered around the room but saw no indication of a struggle. Was it a robbery? He checked the cash drawer but nothing had been taken. He turned to William's entry book. The last recorded train was a freight train going east at 12:15 a.m., approximately twenty minutes prior to his alarming phone call. Who killed Stone?

Then the chief discovered a bloody handprint on one of the cabinets. Stone's hands were clean of blood. Could this be the handprint of the killer?

As news of the murder spread, speculation abounded. A call went out to Ontario Provincial Police Inspector William Greer.

Two leads led to dead ends. When Stone's sister reported having had a dream the week before her brother's death in which she had seen him shot at work in the same manner as the actual crime, the mystery deepened.

An inquest began in January 1915, and continued intermittently until June, when another shocking event took place. William Stone Sr., the murder victim's father, arrived home late on the evening of June 18, somewhat under the influence. He felt he had become a suspect.

Stone Sr. had been called as a witness at the inquest, and he had assumed that he was now the target of the investigation. He was sure the authorities were linking him to his son's murder. Unable to bear it, Billy's father set out that night to end his life. At the Grand Trunk Railway, not far from the scene of the crime, he lay down on the tracks and chose death. Had he murdered his own son?

It was plausible. William Stone Sr. did have a reputation as a heavy drinker and had faced charges of assault to his daughter while under the influence. He had even threatened to kill her. Had he killed his son for insurance money?

Harry Birmingham, a close friend of William Stone Jr., had been the last known person to see him before his death. Birmingham claimed he had left the station at 11:30 p.m. on the night of the murder. Birmingham had apparently said that he and Stone had also been fired at in a field by Corbett's Crossing. Birmingham, however, denied this story at the inquest.

Two bus drivers, who had often chatted with the victim when they arrived at the station to pick up passengers, testified that one, and sometimes two, revolvers were kept in the drawer of Stone's desk. Were the revolvers in the desk drawer on the night of the murder? The police found no revolvers in the drawer. Birmingham owned an old revolver, but the .38-calibre bullet that killed Stone did not fit his gun. Birmingham was cleared.

Brian Winters, Whitby's historical archivist, once recalled this story in the local paper and he had something to add, "One Whitby resident recalls that, many years later, in the 1920s or 30s a man was executed in the United States. As the trap door dropped, he confessed to a murder in Whitby. But it was too late to find out what murder it was, for he was dead before he could complete what he was saying."

The murder of Billy Stone remains unsolved. Who left their bloody handprint at the scene of the crime? Does Billy haunt the old train station today?

INTERESTING RESIDENTS

SHERIFF NELSON REYNOLDS

There may not have been the likes of Wyatt Earp in Ontario, but there was Sheriff Nelson Reynolds.

He was an adventuresome fellow, his appearance dignified. He sported thick, curly hair and sideburns that brushed the lapels of his jacket. He was a spiritual person in essence, but still very aware of personal glory and of his own self-righteous goals

To many he was known simply as the Sheriff. Few knew that in his youth he had been a treasonable participant in the Rebellion of Upper Canada or that in his later years he would be a man who would build the castle of his dreams.

Reynolds was born in 1814. He led his own cavalry regiment in Kingston when the rebellion of 1837 broke out. Government officials kept a watchful eye on Reynolds who never hid his criticism of those in power. They were leery of him, worried that instead of leading his troops in defence of the city against attacking patriots, he might turn and join the opposing forces.

On the eve of February 1837, a false alarm was sounded warning of the invasion by patriotic forces. Officials, convinced that this would be the night for Reynolds to turn patriotic, ordered government troops to surround Reynolds and his men and to charge their commanding officer with high treason. Before Reynolds could lead a charge he and his men were captured. Reynolds refused arrest and stood his ground until a musket cracked and a lead ball found its mark in his leg. Fearing for his life and with the help of his men, he broke free and escaped across the American border. It was not until July of 1838 that he returned and surrendered to government officials. He was led under guard to Fort Henry where he was imprisoned and charged with high treason.

At his trial, Reynolds conducted his own defence, where he set out to prove his innocence. By this time, even Lord Durham had heard the formal pleas of this officer and had travelled to visit him in his jail cell. The trial took place and Reynolds proved his innocence, through a lack of evidence.

With the news of his release, the soldiers from his former regiment rushed to meet him, rejoicing his freedom by carrying him through the streets of Kingston on their shoulders.

Fourteen years later, in 1854, he was appointed Sheriff of Ontario County. His duties included land arrangements, the signing of legal documents, and foreclosure on mortgages.

His lifelong dream was to build a castle and build one he did. Sheriff Reynolds began construction of Trafalgar Castle at the east end of Dundas Street in Whitby, Ontario.

Trafalgar Castle, the former home of Sheriff Nelson Reynolds. It became the Ontario Ladies' College, and is now known as the Trafalgar Castle School.

Because he hoped to attract royalty, he spared no cost in its construction. Upon completion, his elegant castle, entirely built of stone, stood as a monument to fine craftsmanship. One could even imagine they were standing in the English countryside when they gazed at this dwelling.

And his dream of attracting royalty did come true. In 1864 Prince Arthur III, son of Queen Victoria and later the governor general of Canada, visited the sheriffs' castle. Sir John A. Macdonald, never one to turn down a dinner invitation, also visited the castle.

Sadly, in 1874, the purse strings drew to a close. Elegance and extravagance had cost him his castle. Although forced to sell his dream, Sheriff Reynolds never lost sight of his vision. The moment Trafalgar Castle was sold, Reynolds built again. After all, one does need considerable space when they have fathered twenty-four children. This time his castle was a smaller replica of his former home. At the age of sixty-seven he slept his last night in his castle and was buried in Whitby.

Sheriff Reynold's second home had a succession of ownership including fine dining in the 1980s. Today, it is a Montessori School — a proud heritage for the Sheriff.

JOSEPH BIGELOW

Every town owes its prosperity in some part to individual men and women who at crucial stages have had visions — visions that have led them to use their own private fortunes to overcome opposition from more cautious elements in their communities and brought prosperity for all.

Often their efforts were not appreciated by the people, particularly if they themselves prospered as a result of their ideas.

One such man was Joseph Bigelow. Born in 1829, one of ten sons of Hiram Bigelow of Simcoe County, he moved with the family to Lindsay in 1844. In 1851, Joseph and his twin brother Joel moved to Port Perry where they opened a general store under the name of J & J Bigelow. Joel soon moved on to Whitby and later to Chicago.

During his active years Joseph was involved financially and other-wise, in important improvement in the Port Perry and Scugog area. He was the first postmaster in Port Perry from 1852 to 1869. In the late 1850s he took over a woollen factory and planing mill from J.C. Bowerman and Company, who had operated them on the site of the old railway engine sheds near the present-day yacht club.

In 1862, a branch of the Royal Canadian Bank opened in Port Perry with Mr. Bigelow as manager. He retired from this position in 1868 to pursue the construction of a three-storey commercial emporium called the Royal Arcade.

Bigelow's next project was the construction of the Port Whitby and Port Perry Railway. He was the chief instigator and advocate and insisted that such a line to the Grand Trunk system would be advantageous to the business of the town. He, along with Thomas Paxton, C.E. English, and James Dryden, invested money into the project. When the railway became a reality they withdrew most of their investment and passed control to Mr. James Austin, president of the Dominion Bank in Toronto; James Michie, a merchant of Toronto; and James Holden of Whitby.

The first council of Port Perry met in 1872. Joseph Bigelow was reeve. He continued to serve office until 1874.

In 1877 he became a Justice of the Peace and the new owner of an elaborate house, designed and built by H.R. Barber of Oshawa. The interior was equally elaborate, with heavy trim, archways, and a grand staircase prominently placed in a generous foyer. There was a summer kitchen in the full-sized basement and the winter kitchen was situated at the rear of the house. The drawing room, reception room, dining room, and domestic offices were on the first floor, with bedrooms and maids' quarters on the second. Joseph had several fireplaces with marbleized-slate

Author's Collection.

In 1877, Joseph Bigelow became the owner of an elaborate Italianate house designed and built by H.R. Barber.

mantelpieces built throughout the house, but his wife refused to allow fires to be lit, arguing that a fireplace dirtied, rather than heated, a home. Joseph was forced to seal them off.

The Bigelow house, situated on Cochrane Street in Port Perry, is well worth a look today. It is still a splendid brick home with iron casting to the flat decks of the roof, a tower, a bay window and a decorative verandah that have all survived the years.

Joseph Bigelow's political career was short lived. He ran for the Ontario Legislature in 1881, but lost by three votes. Nonetheless, he continued to promote and establish business in Port Perry.

When Joseph Bigelow died in 1917, at the regal age of eighty-nine, flags flew at half-mast on public buildings to pay tribute to a man whose vision and spirit enabled him to manifest his dreams, an inspiration to all.

GEORGE REID, THE PAINTER

For fifty years George Reid was one of the outstanding artists of this country. He was active in every artistic movement that materialized in Toronto, and the rest of Canada, from the 1890s. He had a wide range of interests up to the autumn of 1885, and did not specialize, although this could be called his portrait period. From 1885 to 1895 he was a painter of scenes of Canadian life. In his next period he explored his interest in murals.

As a painter of historical subjects he was second only to C.W. Jefferys. The greatest number of landscape paintings came between 1925 and 1935. His mural work was his greatest single contribution to Canadian art and it was in his second mural period, 1925 to 1938, that he really established himself as a muralist.

George Reid was born near Wingham, Ontario, in 1860. During his first years in school, he developed an interest in history and drawing, and at the age of ten he announced that he was going to be a painter. His father discouraged him and apprenticed him to J.B. Proctor, an architect and the owner of a planing mill in Wingham, for three years. This gave another facet to his career and also brought him fame. Luckily for Reid, Proctor's business waned, and he was released from his contract.

Reid went to Toronto and enrolled in night-school lessons at the Toronto School of Art. He tried to find a job related to his studies but he was forced to take a job in a machine shop to support himself.

He returned to Wingham to open a portrait studio. He boarded with his cousin, Frank Buchanan. He painted portraits of the Buchanan family, and this brought him more clients. One of his portraits was of C. Tait Scott, a Wingham banker. He told his friends in Kincardine, who in turn invited Reid to open a studio there, when business fell off in Wingham. By the time he was twenty-one years of age he had a sizeable bank account.

Since there were no courses in life drawing/painting in Toronto, he left for Philadelphia to study at the Academy of Fine Arts. There, he met Mary, another student, and later they were married. They spent their honeymoon in Europe, touring art galleries. When the returned to Toronto, Reid gave art lessons and their two-room flat became open house for many artists.

In 1890, when Toronto city hall was being built, Reid recommended that the city commission artists to decorate the wall with murals. The city, however, would not spend the money. In later years, Reid painted the two large murals in the main lobby that show the arrival of the first pioneers, at no charge. In his sixties and seventies he painted a large mural for the auditorium of Jarvis Street Collegiate and for one of the galleries that is now the library of the Royal Ontario Museum.

In 1906, he was made President of the Royal Canadian Academy and the one, consuming aim of his life became the establishment of a permanent art school in Canada.

Following his death, the Wingham town council asked Mrs. Reid for a copy of his work called *Burning of the Mortgage*. It was not available but she did donate a piece named *Coming of the White Man*. This now hangs in the Wingham and District Historical Museum. In October 1954, Mrs. Reid gave another painting to the town, *Indian Bartering Furs*. It hangs in the Wingham Public Library.

During his life, George Reid donated upwards of four hundred of his paintings to the Ontario government for use in public buildings and for schools in Ontario.

FRANKLIN AND THE
NORTHWEST PASSAGE

Beginning nearly three hundred years ago, before Sir John Franklin sought to chart a route to the riches of China and East India, a seventeenth-century Cambridge scholar, William Watts, compared the quest for a Northwest Passage with the legendary voyage of Jason and the Argonauts. He noted that Jason had found his Golden Fleece, while the Northwest Passage represented the search, but not the find.

None of the early sixteenth-century expeditions of Martin Frobisher and John Davis succeeded in locating an open Polar Sea and trade route across the top of North America. In 1619, Danish naval captain Jens Munk set out with two ships, in search of the Northwest Passage. Forced to winter at the mouth of the Churchill River, sixty-one of the sixty-four crewmen died from the effects of the extreme cold and scurvy. Munk and two of his men survived.

Nearly a hundred years later, James Knight set sail to look for the Northwest Passage and for a treasure of precious metals he believed lay in Canada's barren Arctic. Knight's expedition vanished and was never seen again. Forty years later another Arctic explorer, Samuel Hearne, discovered what had happened to Knight. Apparently Knight had been shipwrecked on Marble Island where some of the crew members survived for several years before they too succumbed to the cold and scurvy. When only two survivors remained, the Inuit reported observing the men standing at the tip of the island, waiting, perhaps, for a relief expedition. Hearne recorded that the two men had apparently continued there for a considerable time and, when nothing appeared, they sat down together and wept bitterly — one died and the other died in an attempt to dig a grave for his companion.

On the morning of May 19, 1845, two ships left England in search of the Northwest Passage, led by Sir John Franklin. On board, the ships carried enough provisions to last five years. Among the food supplies were 61,987 kilograms of flour, 16,749 litres of liquor, 909 litres of wine for the sick, and nearly 8,000 tins filled with preserved meat, soups, and vegetables.

Franklin's last contact with the outside world came in early August 1845, when they met two whaling ships in Baffin Bay. Captain Martin, commander of the ships was invited to dine with Franklin, but shifting winds set the ships apart. Franklin and crew vanished in the world of ice and snow.

By 1847, England was concerned about the fate of Franklin and sent out three separate expeditions to relieve Sir John Franklin, but they all returned without finding even a trace of him or his ship and crew.

On April 4, 1850, the *Toronto Globe* published the announcement of a reward by Her Majesty's Government "to any party or parties of any country, who shall render efficient assistance to the crews of the discovery ships under the command of Sir John Franklin."

In the autumn of 1850, one ship was combing the Arctic waterways for a sign of the missing explorer. Commander Robert McClure and his crew on the HMS *Investigator* searched the waterways without success. They soon became entrapped in winter ice. Their own safety was in jeopardy. They survived as best they could for three years, while awaiting rescue. Several members of the crew succumbed to illness and the cold.

Despite their situation, Robert McClure and crew continued on foot, looking for Franklin and for the Northwest Passage. Commander McClure and his crew never solved the mystery of the disappearance of Franklin, but they did find the Northwest Passage. The crew of the HMS *Investigator* were eventually rescued and returned safely to England. The commander and surviving crew were awarded medals and shared the reward money for discovering the Northwest Passage.

It wasn't until May 25, 1859, that a human skeleton in the uniform of a steward from the lost expedition was found by a Captain McClintock. A note was found telling of the terrible fate of the Franklin expedition. The note explained that the ships had become trapped in the ice off King William Island for nineteen months. Franklin had died, and the remaining forty crew members began a doomed march for safety, only to die in the cold and snow.

Many questions were raised about how an expedition so well outfitted could end in disaster. Lead poisoning from the tin cans was the answer. The end parts of the seams of the cans were not properly sealed and, as a result, the entire crew perished.

Who could imagine that those many brave explorers who sailed the Arctic waters would return again and settle in Ontario. My great-great-grandfather, Henry Gauen, was one of those men who had served under the command of McClure on the HMS *Investigator* in 1850. Henry Gauen returned and settled in the village of Ivanhoe, Ontario, situated north of Belleville. There he served as the first president of the Ivanhoe Cheese Company, which is still in operation today.

Author's Collection.

Henry Gauen, the author's great-great-grandfather, was an Arctic explorer and a member of the group of men who found the Northwest Passage during the McClure Expedition in search of Franklin.

DAVID BOYLE

David Boyle was born in Scotland in 1842, and was the founding father of modern archaeology in Ontario. His contributions to the theory and practice of Canadian archaeology were great. Despite his immensely innovative and impressive contributions as an archaeologist and his noteworthy work as an educator and museum curator, David Boyle has remained a little-known figure in Canada. He is truly one of the forgotten men of Canada's past.

Who was David Boyle? What kind of a man was he? How did he rise to achieve international renown as the most important single figure in Canadian archaeology prior to the First World War?

David Boyle was the son of a blacksmith who immigrated to Canada in 1856, when David was fourteen years old. David himself apprenticed as a blacksmith in Wellington County from 1857 to 1860. His subsequent transformation from artisan to archaeologist is a remarkable story. According to Gerald Killan in his book entitled *David Boyle*, "It is the odyssey of a self-taught individual who rejected the prevailing materialist values of his day and dedicated himself instead to the ideal of self-culture and to the acquisition and imparting of knowledge."

Initially, the quest for knowledge led him to teaching school, first as the master of a one-room schoolhouse in Upper Pilkington Township, Wellington County, from 1865 to 1871, and later as the principal of the Elora Public School from 1871 to 1881. Boyle emerged, during this period, as a truly innovative and superior nineteenth-century teacher.

Courtesy of the Ontario Archives.

David Boyle, teacher and archaeologist, is responsible for the discovery and preservation of Serpent Mounds on Rice Lake.

He was a man of patience and persistence. He undertook the task of teaching a deaf-mute girl to read and write.

During the 1870s in Elora, Boyle's self-improvement ethic and child-centred educational philosophy resulted in the formation of three cultural institutions: the Elora Mechanic's Institute, the third largest of its kind in Ontario by 1881; the Elora School Museum, which housed one of the best natural science collections in Ontario; and the Elora Natural History Society.

Following brief and unsuccessful stints as a textbook promoter in 1882 and 1883 and a proprietor of Ye Olde Booke Shoppe and Natural Science Exchange in Toronto, he found his place in the world of scholarship. He became the curator/archaeologist of a museum from 1896 to 1911, which was housed in the Toronto Normal School. The important collections were eventually transferred in 1933 to the David Boyle Room of the Royal Ontario Museum.

Boyle's interest in the past Aboriginal occupations of Ontario essentially materialized in the 1870s, during his explorations of the fields and river valleys of Wellington County. He made one of his first artifactual finds during the 1860s, on his uncle's farm near Richmond Hill. His first major excavation occurred on October 5, 1885, when he reinvestigated the historic Neutral ossuaries north-west of Hamilton. These burials had previously been examined in 1836 and in 1843. Boyle obtained enough artifacts to put together an exhibit in the front window of his Toronto bookstore.

Many of the sites he investigated are now classics: Serpent Mounds near Peterborough; the Clearville, Lawson, Parker, and Solid Comfort sites in Southwestern Ontario; Christian Island on Georgian Bay; the Bon Echo pictographs and Beckstead sites in eastern Ontario; and the Nipigon Bay rock paintings north of Superior. David Boyle also produced the first archaeological map of Ontario in 1906.

David Boyle died on February 14, 1911, and was buried in Mount Pleasant Cemetery.

DAVID SUZUKI

Last Saturday night I travelled to Uxbridge to hear Dr. David Suzuki speak about his latest book, *Wisdom of the Elders*. What a night and what a speaker! You could have heard a pin drop as he addressed a crowd of more than two hundred people. He was there to speak to those who care about the planet, who care about the place they call home. Dr. Suzuki was on tour in Ontario to deliver a powerful message.

He began by talking about his many years as a scientist and about how as a young man, he had faith that science would unravel all of the secrets of the universe. After twenty-five years of studying the fruit fly, he realized that scientific discoveries had not led to the improved world he once believed they would. There were, he found, more mysteries than science alone could ever understand or explain.

In spite of amazing strides in science and technology during the late 1960s and early '70s, the planet was showing ever greater signs of stress.

He spoke about the population explosion on the earth in the past 150 years, and the devastating impact that this increase in humanity has had on the planet. Every second, three human beings are born — 250,000 a day, 90 million per year. At the same time, total global food production has been declining since 1984 due to the annual loss of top-soil: 25 billion tons.

A billion people a day go to bed at night not just hungry, but starving, he stated. Of the 45,000 human beings who die every day of starvation, three-quarters are children under the age of five.

After citing high PCB levels, even in remote Baffin Island, Dr. Suzuki said there is not one place left on this earth in pristine condition. Acid rain, ozone layer depletion, CFCs and greenhouse gases have changed the planet's very atmosphere. Wilderness habitats and species are disappearing at frightening rates — species at the rate of fifty thousand per year, according to a Harvard scientist.

Dr. Suzuki stated, "Industrial civilization and the sheer weight of human numbers is now global and is changing the biosphere with frightening speed. It is clear that major problems such as global warming, ozone depletion, species extinction, and worldwide toxic pollution will not be solved in the long run by perpetuating the current worldview, or by applying band-aids, such as tax levies, greater efficiency, and recycling. Knowledge gained through science is unique and profound, yet also extremely limited. Not only do we fail to comprehend the complexity of life on earth, we have barely begun to understand its dimensions."

He told the audience that we needed a radically different way of relating ourselves to the support systems of the planet.

For a moment I looked around the audience to seek out the response from the crowd to such direct statements. What I saw was women and men with their heads lowered and with tears streaming down their cheeks. I turned and focused back on David Suzuki.

"My experiences," he said, "with Aboriginal peoples, have convinced me, both as a scientist and as an environmentalist, of the power and relevance of their traditional knowledge and worldview in a time of imminent, global catastrophe. This was the inspiration for *Wisdom of the Elders*."

Wisdom of the Elders is said to be the first book to explore beliefs about the delicate relationships between humans, nature, and the environment.

David Suzuki believes we must first get in touch with our environment with our hearts instead of our heads. We must connect with the earth at the level of the soil. I agree. How about it?

GERALD SINCLAIR HAYWARD

Few Canadians know much about the famous artist who built his summer home on the shore of Rice Lake, Ontario. On January 20, 1845, one of Canada's most prolific but least-known painters, Gerald Sinclair Hayward, was born. He was a brilliant man of many talents and he explored them all. He was chief engineer aboard a prairie schooner on the Dakota Plains in the early 1860s, and upon returning to Canada he enlisted for frontier service with the Port Hope Infantry Company in November 1865. He was awarded a Queen's medal and discharged in April 1866, with the rank of ensign. His next endeavour involved farming and railroading, but neither seemed to satisfy him. In his early twenties he decided to explore an entirely new career.

The art of painting miniature portraits and scenes appealed to Hayward, but it was not widely practiced in Canada, so he went to study at the Royal Academy schools in London, England in 1870. While there, he was commissioned by many members of the English, German, and Russian courts to do miniature portraits on ivory. He painted Queen Victoria, the Prince of Wales (later King Edward VII), Princess Alice, the Countess of Minto, the Duke and Duchess of Buckingham, Lord and Lady Caven, the Empress of Prussia, and the Czarevitch of Russia. Later in Canada, he painted Prime Ministers MacDonald and Laurier.

Hayward gave the first exhibition of ninety modern miniatures in the United States at the Avery Galleries, New York, in 1889, and continued to exhibit throughout the country. One leading newspaper said: "Mr.

Hayward has become world-famous in his exclusive field and has painted more than a thousand distinguished persons in America on coming out from London."

Another wrote, "His work is strongly individualistic — the eye full of life, hair freely treated, fidelity in time of complexion, with perfect harmony in tone of background, combine to make the living portrait possible to obtain."

Hayward took up residence in New York City, but returned to Ontario to build a summer home in Gores Landing on Rice Lake in 1902. He hired a local builder and craftsman, Fred Pratt, to build a waterfront summer house on the edge of the village. Hayward drew some sketches and requirements for a "single" style home popular along the eastern seaboard of the United States. According to the Victoria Inn website:

> The asymmetrical composition of the structure is somewhat whimsical in appearance. The overall impression is a rather imposing four-bayed frame building of two and a half stories. The main building is forty-five feet by forty-five feet with a full three-storey exterior tower incorporated into the north-east corner verandah and roofline plan. The original plan included first and second level open verandahs running across three sides. The verandahs were eventually closed in. Care has been taken to preserve the earlier interior verandah wainscoting and double French doors. This finely "raised relief trim" appears as a repeated pattern on doors, wainscoting and on the walls of three bedrooms.

He named his home The Willows. It was his favourite retreat, and he was so enchanted with the panoramic view from his tower window that he later painted the lake and its many islands on the walls of his dining room.

As church warden, Hayward assisted in the building of St. George's Anglican Church in the village, and much of its artistic appearance is due to his interest in the construction. When he died in New York on March 31, 1926, his ashes were brought to Gores Landing by his daughter and buried in the cemetery of the church. The *Toronto Star Weekly* published an article on Hayward on April 3, stating, "In the passing of Gerald Sinclair Hayward, world-famous miniature painter, Canada loses one of her greatest artists."

Unfortunately, he has been all but forgotten as a Canadian artist. The murals of Rice Lake on his dining room walls are now covered with two coats of paint, and his beautiful home, The Willows, is now known as Victoria Inn.

GREY OWL

"Man should enter the woods, not with any conquistador obsession or mighty hunter complex, but rather with the awe, and not a little of the veneration, of one who steps within the portals of some vast and ancient edifice of wondrous architecture. For many a man who considers himself the master of all he surveys, would do well, when setting foot in the forest, to take off not only his hat, but his shoes too and, in not a few cases, be glad he is allowed to retain an upright position. For the woods, in time, sometimes a very short time will make either a man or a monkey of you."

This statement was written by a man some will remember and of whom others will never have heard. He was a country, a spirit, a saviour of the beaver, and his name was Grey Owl.

His story begins in his youth, in the years between 1907 and 1924, when he, Archie Belaney, a young English immigrant became internationally famous under the assumed Aboriginal name of Grey Owl. He wandered throughout Northern Ontario and claimed the land radiating from Temagami and Bear Island. His claim, however, was never paid for in cash nor filed legally. Instead, it was staked by a heart and a spirit that were attuned to the wilderness he had discovered, and paid for in sweat and understanding. This was the Aboriginal way, and he later recorded his journey in four published books.

Like any land paid for by the heart and soul rather than the dollar, the precise boundaries of Grey Owl's wilderness were uncharted. He wrote, "All other districts, to me, lack the austere magnificence and rugged grandeur of the highlands of Northern Ontario, with their bold, romantic scenery, uncounted and uncountable deep water lakes and wild rushing rivers."

Because he wished to pass on what he had learned as a Englishman who changed his lifestyle and spirit to live as an Aboriginal person, he gave passionate warnings and made accurate prophecies about many things: the wanton destruction of the forests, the fate of Aboriginal peoples, the pollution and mismanagement of rivers and lakes, the greed of the commercial world and its infringement on the wilderness, the perils of a soft life, man's aesthetic need of the wilderness, and the overwhelming ignorance of Canadians to the obvious fact that Canada's originality lay in its north.

Like most unique writers, Grey Owl was ahead of his time. His essays are more likely to seem pertinent to Canadians of our generation and of generations to come than they ever did to our parents and grandparents. After all, how many Canadians who lived through the Depression — and Grey Owl's books first came out in the early thirties — felt that they needed to be warned about the perils of soft living or about the waste of natural resources?

He wrote:

> We, today, of this generation, are seeing the last of the free trappers, a race of men, who, in passing, will turn the last page in the story of true adventure on this continent and close forever the book of romance in Canadian history. The forest cannot much longer stand before the conquering march of man, and soon we shall witness the vanishing of a mighty wilderness.
>
> And the last frontiersman, offspring of that wilderness, driven back further and further towards the north into the far-flung reaches where only desolation and barrenness, must, like the forest that evolved him, bow his head to the inevitable and perish with it. And he will leave behind him only his deserted, empty trails, and the ashes of his dead camp fires, as landmarks for the oncoming millions. And with him will go his friend the

Indian to be a memory of days and a life that are past beyond recall.

Grey Owl spent his years in the Canadian north living the Ojibwa way of life. He wrote essays about his observations and books of stories relating to a better way of life. He toured continents and autographed his books, attempting to point out to mankind that there was a chance to change this obsession with modernization. "Love nature" was his motto. I believe his writings should be studied in every school in the country.

LOCAL INTEREST

OIL SPRINGS:
THE OIL CAPITAL OF NORTH AMERICA

Loud thundering cracks could be heard across the countryside when thirty oil wells blew and deep crude flowed over the wellheads for days. Before long the rush was on and more than one thousand oil wells laboured under a forest of ash-pole derricks. This was the beginning of Oil Springs, Ontario, the birthplace of the oil industry in North America.

The village of Oil Springs, forty-eight kilometres southeast of Sarnia, was initially surveyed in 1832. One unusual feature of the district was the presence of gum beds covering the surface of Lots 17 and 18. This black oil substance also floated on the waters of a local creek and hence the original name — Black Creek.

In 1851, Charles and Henry Tripp purchased land at Black Creek to collect and distill the dark gum to make asphalt for sealing the hulls of ships. They could also recover lighting fluids. Three years later a charter was granted and the Tripps were in business.

The brothers advertised their plans and attempted to raise the necessary funds to manufacture and transport their goods to market. The public, however, failed to recognize the value of this enterprise. Without funds and without a railway to move the product to market, the Tripps were forced to sell their holdings. James Williams was waiting in the wings. At thirty-nine years of age, he was a manufacturer of fine carriages and railway cars in Hamilton and he purchased the gum beds and other land in the district. According to Nick Mika, author of *Places in Ontario*, "Williams, who dug the first well, devised a means of refining the oil to produce kerosene, then very much in demand as a light fuel."

Williams tried chopping and boiling the gum product, but eventually decided to drill. To his surprise, at fourteen feet he struck oil. He soon began to pump fifty barrels a day and knew the next step was to build a refinery.

By 1856, Williams was operating five wells and yielding six hundred to eight hundred gallons of oil a day. By the end of the year he had pumped approximately three hundred thousand gallons of oil. With this he drew the attention of the world.

In 1858 Williams had a productive well and refinery, and was also shipping to a broader market, changing the lives of millions of people.

Michael O'Meara, in a booklet about Oil Springs, told the story. "From every part of Canada and United States men came with cash and equipment, the drillers, farmhands, teamsters, blacksmiths, leeches and rogues. They rode, drove and walked to the rich gum beds through the flat, undrained swamp. Shacks mushroomed without pattern in their clutter of equipment."

The first commercial oil well in North America began operation in 1858 in Oil Springs.

Black Creek exploded with activity. The village was brightly lit with fluid lamps, and horse-drawn buses gave twenty-four hour service at five-minute intervals. There were nine hotels, several saloons, and twelve general stores. A new plank road connected the oil capital of the world to Port Sarnia. Stagecoaches travelled the road four times a day.

In 1861 Hugh Shaw arrived in Black Creek with fifty dollars in his pocket and title to one acre of land. Shaw was determined to become rich. He had already been terminated out of partnership in experimental drilling at nearby Petrolia. Determined to strike out he began drilling on his property in July. Month after month went by. By December he was broke. He had drilled into bedrock without any success. People began to mock his efforts. No one had ever drilled that deep before and discovered oil.

At fifty years old he felt beaten, discouraged, and discarded, but he made a promise to himself that he would try just one more day before abandoning the hole.

On January 16, 1862, Shaw drilled one more foot and a loud crack resounded from the bottom of the well and across the entire field. Moments later a heavy, thick oil shot up to tree-top level. The first gusher had blown. Soon hundreds of thousands of barrels of oil flooded the fifty-acre basin one to three feet deep. There seemed no way to control the flow. Shaw even wrapped a flax-filled leather bag around the bottom of a two and a half inch pipe and stuffed it down the three inch bore of the well. This helped, but still the oil gushed twenty feet high, producing five hundred barrels of oil a day. The flow was so strong that thirty five-gallon barrels could be filled in a minute and three-quarters.

By now oil flowed a foot thick in the waters of Black Creek. Soon the black slick covered the western part of Lake St. Clair. Shaw eventually controlled the gusher by installing a three-quarter inch pipe that extended twenty feet above the ground. By the end of that year one thousand wells in Oil Springs were producing twelve thousand barrels a day. Oil sold for ten dollars a barrel.

A post office was opened under the name of Oil Springs; the population of the village exceeded three thousand, six refineries were operating in the oil fields, and a Chicago firm was proposing to build a 108-room hotel.

In 1862, 1000 oil wells in Oil Springs were producing 12,000 barrels of oil a day.

Courtesy of the Ontario Archives.

Meanwhile Bernard King struck oil in Petrolia, eleven kilometres north of Oil Springs. Petrolia would quickly replace Oil Springs as Canada's oil capital.

Alas, the oil boom in Oil Springs did not last. According to the Oil Museum of Canada, "The great surge of oil from Oil Springs, coupled with increased United States production, helped to deflate the price of oil to less than one dollar a barrel. At the same time, production from the big flowing wells began to diminish, and worn-out refining equipment was not replaced. Many oil producers and merchants literally moved their homes and shops to Petrolia. Freshly drilled wells with steady oil flow were more attractive than Oil Springs' dried-up gushers. The population of Oil Springs fell to 550.

"In the early1880s, the price of oil rose and revived crude production in Oil Springs for a time. By 1898, production reached 133,000 barrels per year, but the size and grandeur of the original boom was never repeated."

Today Oil Springs features two hundred wells in operation, pumping twenty-six thousand barrels a year. Many of these wells are still owned by the Fairbanks family, whose ancestors participated in the first oil boom of Oil Springs.

According to some experts, only 35 percent of the Oil Springs fields potential have been recovered. This may mean that twenty million barrels of oil still lie in the limestone crevices and pockets of Mother Earth.

Visitors to Oil Springs today can actually participate in a driving tour of the oil fields. It is a delightful trip to view some of the original equipment, sheds, and rigs still standing throughout the countryside. The Oil Museum of Canada is worth a visit as well. There you can learn the details and unique history of the "oil boom."

COLLINGWOOD

Collingwood was originally known as Hen and Chickens Harbour, an apt description of the one large and four small offshore islands off Georgian Bay that have since become part of the mainland. The mainland was covered with dense bush, tangled tamaracks, and a cedar swamp. The locality seemed so uninviting that there was no thought of developing a town at Hen and Chickens Harbour until the railway engineers chose it to be the northern terminus of the Ontario, Simcoe, and Huron Railway. This line linked Toronto on Lake Ontario to the waters of Lake Huron. The railway was renamed the Northern Railway of Canada in 1858.

The first settler to arrive in the area was George Carney, in 1835, and he was followed by Joel Underwood, an American, in 1847.

In 1852, Underwood purchased 335 acres of land, across from the "hen and her chicks." He supplied the land for the erection of a steam sawmill, a business that became the economic nucleus for the future city.

Collingwood had been the name of a township in Simcoe County, a tribute to the English admiral Lord Cuthbert Collingwood, and now the name given to this new settlement.

Work progressed on a pier and a breakwater in the harbour. The settlement grew so quickly that it was incorporated as a town in 1858, without ever having been incorporated as a village. The activities of the town reflected the hurried pace of development. Hector McAllister built Collingwood's first boat and Andrew Lockerbee built the machine

Author's Collection.

In 1870, the largest grain elevator on the Great Lakes was built in Collingwood. In 1882, Collingwood used debentures to the amount of twenty-five thousand dollars to assist in building and establishing a dry dock and a shipbuilding yard in the harbour.

shops for their repair. Numerous mills and hotels sprang up around the town. In 1870, the largest grain elevator on the Great Lakes was built at Collingwood. In 1882, Collingwood issued debentures to assist in building and establishing a dry dock and a shipbuilding yard in town.

Several fires had occurred in the town at different times, but the one on Sunday, September 25, 1881, was the most disastrous of them all. The fire swept through a large portion of Hurontario Street (the main thoroughfare) in the business section of the town.

Steamships figured prominently in the life of Collingwood and other Great Lake ports. Majestic and increasingly palatial vessels like the luxurious J.B. Maxwell, a paddlewheeler with tall stacks, wood-panelled staterooms, and a grand dining salon, made runs from Midland and Penetanguishene to Parry Sound. Luxury liners with grand names — such as the *City of Midland*, and much later the *City of Parry Sound*, *City of Collingwood*, *Majestic City of Toronto*, and several others — were the glory of this inland sea. They were capable of accommodating up to one thousand passengers in style and comfort.

In 1946, a Czechoslovakian refugee by the name of Jozo Weider arrived in Collingwood. This native of mountainous central Europe turned his attention to Blue Mountain. In a short time he built a ski area that now covers a thousand acres. His second love in life was pottery, and with skiing underway, he devoted his energies to this industry. Collingwood became the "Pottery Capital of Canada," with six factories turning out products that are internationally known and popular, as Blue Mountain Pottery.

In December 1939, the newly formed Canadian War Supply Board asked for tenders for the building of corvettes (small naval escort vessels) and minesweepers in Canada. Two months later contracts were approved with twelve Canadian companies, including Collingwood Shipyards Limited. The board authorized the building of three flower-class corvettes in 1940, and another five the following year. The price was set at $528,000 per vessel and, as a result, there was increased employment and economic prosperity for Collingwood. More than two hundred steel ships had sailed out of the Collingwood Bay Shipyards to various watery destinies.

The winds blow from a different direction in Collingwood today. Gone are the days of the steamer. The harbour is quieter and the mountain in the distance is busier. People have become a major industry of Collingwood. The hurried pace of tourists in motion have replaced the softer rhythms of ships and the deliberate trot of horses.

SARNIA

It was once a fur trading post named The Rapids; now it is a city named Sarnia. Its origins go back to the arrival of Ignace Cazelet in 1807. In those days this settlement by the St. Clair River consisted of a few log shanties owned by a handful of French settlers and traders. The land was Chippewa hunting territory governed by Chief Puckinans and later by his son, Chief Wawanosh. The French leased the land from the Chippewas until 1827, when the Chippewas surrendered their lands in exchange for a reserve.

Jean Baptiste settled there in 1808 and built on the site where the public library stands today. Shortly thereafter, Father Fluette established himself here to minister to the Roman Catholics along the river.

One of the first English-speaking settlers was Lieutenant Richard E. Vidal, in 1832. The lieutenant had been interested in the possibilities of seaway traffic since 1816, when he first visited The Rapids while in the service. He immediately established a trade route from this point on the St. Clair River across to Detroit.

Although he was a daring and enterprising young man, he soon learned that he was not the only settler who was innovative. During one of his visits to England, the Ferguson family, a family of eight, used his new home. The Fergusons perceived a need for a tavern in the settlement, and decided to adapt the Vidal home for this purpose during his absence. Upon his return the lieutenant discovered the changes made to his property and evicted the Fergusons without ceremony.

Sarnia had its fair share of influential settlers. There was George Durand, who operated a small dry goods store and became the first postmaster, in 1837. And there was Malcolm Cameron, who established himself at about the same time, in the lumbering business and eventually in ship building and shipping itself, from the natural harbour that existed there.

When the population exceeded eight hundred, in 1856, the settlement was incorporated as the Town of Sarnia. The Great Western Railway was in operation by then and that helped to determine Sarnia's importance as a trade centre. The discovery of oil and subsequent establishment of a refinery in 1871 assisted greatly in the growth of the settlement. Between 1880 and 1907, more than one hundred and fifty oil wells came into operation.

In 1890, Sarnia was linked up to Port Huron, Michigan, by a railway tunnel beneath the St. Clair River. When it was completed in 1891, this 1,837-metre tunnel was considered to be one of the finest engineering feats in the world. It operated until 1994.

On May 7, 1914, Sarnia became a city. People foresaw the incredible growth of the petro-chemical industry that did eventually concentrate here. The products manufactured there over the years include, urethane foam, oil-furnace carbon black for use in the rubber industry, anhydrous ammonia, dry and liquid fertilizer materials, liquid petroleum gas, styrene, and a host of chemical, plastic, and pharmaceutical items.

From 1972 to 1978, a billion dollars was spent on new and expanded plants, which employed seven thousand construction workers. From 1982 to 1984, further plant expansions costing another billion were carried out by four thousand workers.

The history of Sarnia seems always to have been rooted in natural soil. The Aboriginal peoples and fur trappers obtained their sustenance from the surface of the land, while later settlers sought what was below the surface.

LONDON

Many people find it hard to imagine that the grand city of London once appeared as a pine-crowned bluff overlooking the valley of the Thames. It was not until 1826 that settlement took place at the forks on the river. Malcolm Burwell was instructed by the government to survey a town plot in the London Township. Building lots were offered to settlers on condition that they pay thirty dollars for the patent and build a small house on the property.

Peter McGregor was the first to arrive and construct a dwelling in the fall of 1826, on Lot 21, South King Street. His log shanty doubled as a home and tavern. He sold whiskey to travellers from a jug over the stump of a tree situated by the front door.

The judicial centre of the London district was moved from Viittoria, near Lake Erie, to London when the courthouse and jail burned in 1825. In London the original frame structure was replaced by a brick edifice in 1830, while the original building became a school. The new courthouse was a replica of Malahide Castle near Dublin, Ireland, the ancestral home of Colonel Thomas Talbot. He was the founder of the Talbot settlement and owned close to fifty thousand acres of land in the London area. The building was renovated in 1880 and remains standing today.

As a judicial centre, the town grew and Dennis O'Brien built the first brick building on the northwest of Rideout and Dundas Streets. It was here that the first barracks were housed. Framed barracks were constructed in 1839 for the British troops sent to Canada to protect

The London courthouse is a replica of Malahide Castle, near Dublin, Ireland.

against border raids following the rebellion of 1837–38. These barracks were located on the present site of Victoria Park. The military played an important role during the early years of London. Eventually, the military reserve occupied eight square blocks.

In 1840, London became an incorporated police village. Just as the settlement seemed to be prospering quite well, fire struck on Sunday April 13, 1845. The fire, fed by westerly winds off the river, quickly engulfed every building on the black bounded by Dundas, King, Talbot, and Rideout Streets. Before nightfall, more than two hundred buildings lay in ashes. The village board of police passed a by-law prohibiting the erection of any more frame buildings within the village limits. The citizens of London went to work rebuilding a village of brick. Two years later, on July 28, 1847, London officially became a town, and six years later a city.

London soon prospered. Carling and Labatt's breweries were well established and the University of Western Ontario was incorporated by an Act of Legislature in 1878. London had become a microcosm of Canadian life — the headquarters of large life insurance and trust companies, the seat of the Anglican Diocese of Huron, and the Roman Catholic Diocese of London. By the late 1880s the manufacture of cigars had become a booming local industry. There were no less than ten firms producing different brands of cigars.

On June 18, 1923, the Honourable Ernest Charles Drury, premier of Ontario, laid the cornerstones for the arts building and the natural science building of the University of Western Ontario. By 1924, Western had its own 225-acre campus and more than forty thousand books in their library.

In the field of medicine, London has long occupied a prominent position among cities of the western hemisphere. It was Doctor George Edward Hall of the Royal Canadian Air Forces who carried out special research in aviation medicine at the University of Western Ontario. Dr. Hall's pioneering study of the effects of gravity on the human body led to the development of pressure suits for the future of aeronautics and astronautics. Dr. Hall was associated with Sir Frederick Banting, who was a lecturer at the Western medical school when he made his initial discovery of insulin in 1921.

Attractions for visitors today are manifold. Storybook Gardens is a 350-acre site in Springbank Park that creates a fantasy land from fairy tales and nursery rhymes. At Richmond and Simcoe Streets stands the Labatt's Pioneer Brewery, a replica of the 1828 brewery, and it features authentic brewing equipment of the past.

From its humble beginnings, London and the surrounding area has blossomed into a prosperous city that is vibrant and alive.

SOUTHAMPTON

The early history of the Southampton area and of the Saugeen River goes back to a time before the arrival of settlers when the Ojibwa and Iroquois feuded over trading territory.

The two nations allowed one another peaceful trading trips to Montreal until bands of Iroquois waylaid several returning parties of Ojibwa all at once. Because it was the fall of the year and already too late in the season to commence warlike operations, retaliation was put off until the following spring and allies were gathered. In the month of the following May, combined forces gathered in two parties, one at Lake St. Clair, the other at Sault Ste. Marie. Seven hundred canoes were assembled at the Sault and those were divided into two groups. One group advanced on the Iroquois by way of the Ottawa Valley and one proceeded to Penetanguishene. At the same time, the Lake St. Clair division came up the east coast of Lake Huron to the mouth of the Saugeen River. A fierce battle ensued. The Iroquois fled before the onslaught of the Ojibwa. The Ojibwa retained possession of these territories until they were surrendered by treaty to the Crown. Then the settlers arrived.

The year was 1831. The location of the fishing party was among the group of islands called the Fishing Islands, in Lake Huron, near a shore of land soon to become the settlement of Southampton.

A man stationed in a tree looked out anxiously, over the nearer part of the lake. He was watching for a shoal of whitefish. In a short time they would appear like a bright cloud moving rapidly through the water. The announcement of their approach would fill each member of the camp of fishermen with a spirit of excitement and energetic activity. A large row boat, the stern piled high with netting, would be quickly manned.

Under the lusty strokes of the crew, the boat moved forward. Reaching a site, the men quickly dropped the net so as to encircle the shoal. There in a small area were thousands and thousands of fish, enough to fill five hundred to a thousand barrels. The net would then be drawn to shore and the fish brought onto the beach. The catch at times was so immense that the landing of fish was extended over three days, to make time for curing.

The beginning of settlement at Southampton began with Captain John Spence and Captain William Kennedy. Both men had been in the employment of the Hudson's Bay Company and retired in 1847. They had originally taken up residence in Kingston, Ontario, but having heard about the profits to be made in the Lake Huron fisheries, they decided to investigate the possibilities. When they arrived at the mouth of the Saugeen River the following year, they erected a log house. Captain Kennedy remained there until 1852, when, at the request of Lady Franklin, he took charge of a party in search of her husband, Sir John Franklin, the Arctic explorer who had not returned.

By 1955, no lake trout were to be found in Lake Huron. The commercial fishing industry in Southampton was finished. The decline of fishing saw the growth of tourism. The wide main street with speciality shops and dining facilities cater to this change in the economic base of the town.

By 1857, one hundred and thirty houses marked the size of the village. In all, there were six shops, two hotels, and five warehouses. A planing mill stood on the beach near a mineral water spring and a steam sawmill sat at the river's edge.

In 1855 the fishing industry of Southampton employed seventy men, manning eighteen boats, amounting to thirty thousand dollars in capital investment.

Fire struck the village in the early morning of November 4, 1886. It started in the house of J.M. Kelly and soon spread through the downtown core. From there it continued eastward, and within four hours everything for two blocks was burned to the ground. More than fifty buildings were consumed and thirty families were left homeless. The losses amounted to sixty thousand dollars.

Places did recover, and in 1904, Southampton was readily and eligible for town status.

Today Southampton offers visitors the opportunity to participate in various sports and events. Many tourists choose to explore the town and study the cultural heritage of the land. Miles of excellent sandy beaches provide ample opportunity to stroll the Huron shoreline and view wonderful sunsets. Southampton reminds me of Myrtle Beach, South Carolina, by the ocean, but without the crowds and hotels lining the waterfront.

Southampton still remains one of those unspoiled settings in Ontario.

PENRYN, PORT HOPE

While the pioneers on land cleared a path through virgin timberland to allow for new settlement, other pioneers fought to secure the waterways to ensure the safe passage of others. One of the latter was Commander John Tucker Williams.

Commander Williams was born in 1789, and left Cornwall, England, at the early age of twelve to join the Royal Navy, where he served as midshipman under Nelson at Copenhagen in 1801. A draft of naval officers came to Kingston, Ontario, in May 1813, for military service, and Lieutenant Williams was among them.

He served in the Lower Lakes until 1816, when he was transferred from the HMS *Netley* to the Upper Lakes. In October of that year he was appointed commander of the schooner *Surprise.*

The following year Commander Williams retired from the navy and left for England, but returned to Upper Canada one year later, bringing with him a dispatch from the Earl of Bathurst to the Duke of Richmond authorizing a grant of land to be given to him, John Tucker Williams, in proportion to his rank. He received, by patent from the Crown, a number of properties in the county of Durham, and in 1829 he established a homestead on one hundred acres of land in Port Hope. He named the house Penryn, after the village in which his parents had been married in England in the late 1700s.

The house was built of lumber from his own property, which was milled on the Ganaraska, then known as Smith's Creek. The bricks for the fireplaces and chimneys were made in Port Hope. At a later date the entire house was bricked over, a square tower replaced the portico, and balcony, and the fanlight (a small, semi-circular window over a door) was removed. A wing on the west end was built, bay windows added, and the window sashes changed. Two octagonal summerhouses that were built on the grounds remain standing today, although in new locations.

Of special interest is the oval room built off the upstairs landing at the head of the fine staircase. Commander Williams built the room to be a replica of a ship's aft cabin. It has a gently sloping deck, and the original stairway was a central gangway, rising from the center of the main hallway. There was an exceedingly fine ship's baluster, which was subsequently removed.

The summer kitchen in the basement, complete with hearth and bake oven, had a cobblestone floor. To the left of this kitchen is a small room with a bookcase against the wall. When the bookcase is pulled gently, it swings out to reveal a hidden vault where important papers and jewels were once stored.

In 1841, Williams ran for the Parliament of Upper Canada to represent the united counties of Durham and Northumberland. His campaign met with success and one of his first acts as a member was to introduce a bill that became law; the first bill to grant copyright for published material in Canada.

He held office until 1848, and in 1850 became the first mayor of Port Hope. He died four years later at the age of sixty-five.

The Penryn estate is one of Port Hope's oldest homes, and it is still maintained as a private residence.

THE DREAM OF OWNING A CASTLE

The dream of owning a castle begins for many as sand castles on the ocean shores. Sir Henry Mill Pellatt, born in 1859, in Kingston, Ontario, knew his castle in the light of reality, only to lose it in the changing tide of fortune.

Sir Henry was only seventeen and already had a shrewd business mind when he joined his father in the stockbroking business. He made a fortune investing in the Northwest Land Company, because he foresaw a time when the west would open up for development.

By 1905, he had made frequent visits to Britain and continental Europe, always collecting sketches and details of magnificent castles that appealed to him. As in the days of King Arthur, Sir Henry, a knight, required a castle and a castle he did build.

Construction of Casa Loma began in 1911, and was completed in 1914. Stone masons from Scotland were employed to build the ninety-room castle, with its intricately carved fireplaces, stately towers, exquisite windows, and detailed doorways, styled after those in Europe.

The interior was a salute to overindulgence with its European hand-loomed tapestries, hand-wrought silver, original oils, uniquely woven rugs, and stylish furnishings. The library was built to accommodate one hundred thousand volumes. The elaborate drawing room was panelled in fine French oak.

Lady Pellatt's suite measured three thousand square feet and included sitting rooms, a bedroom, a sunroom, and a bathroom done in soft-toned Italian marble with gold-plated fixtures.

The castle was set on twenty-five acres surrounded by four hundred varieties of trees, shrubs, and plants and had its own private telephone system, a fountain in the palm room, and a marble swimming pool. An underground tunnel ran from the basement under the road to the horse stables.

Sir Henry decided to venture into real estate to recoup some of his money. With the advent of war, people were forced to invest their sums in war bonds and in industry. Sir Henry slowly lost his fortune and his empire collapsed. Weary of the expense of maintaining Casa Loma, he turned his castle over to the city in 1924. A public auction was held and the treasures of Sir Henry Pellatt were sold to the highest bidder.

In 1937, the Kiwanis's Club of West Toronto Inc. struck an agreement with the city to restore and operate Casa Loma as a tourist attraction. During the 1950s the Kiwanis Club hosted great social parties, offering the finest entertainment around.

Today the great doors of Casa Loam still remain open to the public who wish to catch a glimpse of one man's dream.

Sir Henry was not unlike Sir William McKenzie, a railroad baron of Canada who resided in Kirkfield, Ontario. He also built a mansion displaying an era of wealth and dreams. Unfortunately, he also lost his fortune.

Gerald Sinclair Hayward, one of Canada's finest painters, built his dream home, Victoria Inn, in Gores Landing, Rice Lake. Like Sir Henry Pellatt and Sir William McKenzie, Hayward's dream also faded from memory and his belongings and treasured items were discovered in a barn in New York State in the 1960s and auctioned off for next to nothing.

Samuel Nesbitt, of Brighton, and his home the Whitehouse, changed from a miniature castle with large parties to become a private home and an antique business. Sheriff Nelson Reynolds of Whitby built his castle, Trafalgar, which he lost for financial reasons and became a private girls' school.

Perhaps all castle dreams are plagued by the "curse of sand castles" — high tide.

RAVENSWORTH, COBOURG

At one time it was said that every admiral in the American navy had vacationed at least once in Cobourg, Ontario.

Many of these dignitaries were old army friends of Colonel Chambliss, who loved Cobourg and who encouraged his friends to come up for a vacation during the summer. He had moved to Cobourg to take over the Marmora Mining Railway Company. His father-in-law, George K. Shoenberger, was an American steel capitalist and had become interested in the mining industry in Marmora, Ontario, during 1865.

As the years passed, a number of wealthy American steel capitalists from Pittsburgh arrived in this resort area. Old Cobourg residences were bought and enlarged, and other palatial homes were erected by the incoming barons, in true Newport style.

In 1902, General Charles Lake Fitzhugh built Ravensworth, a summer home, on the shore of Lake Ontario in Cobourg. He was born in Oswego, New York, on August 22, 1838, and he decided to embark on a military career and entered West Point Academy. Little did he know his career would begin when the Civil War broke out in 1860.

Charles Fitzhugh at once gave his services to his country. He was commissioned as first lieutenant for the northern army in the field of artillery. There was little delay before his unit was in action and had fought in several engagements. Later, he was appointed to colonel by New York State and served in the cavalry. On the battlefield he proved his worth and Charles Fitzhugh soon became the youngest general in the northern army.

Ravensworth, a summer home built by General Charles Fitzhugh, was once the scene of an attempted assassination.

Fitzhugh married Emma Shoenberger in 1865 and resigned from the army in 1867. He went to work in the steel industry for the firm Shoenberger and Company, just at the time when George Shoenberger had begun operations in Marmora.

Charles Fitzhugh purchased seventy-five acres in Cobourg by Lake Ontario. There he built Ravensworth, his summer home where he lived until his death in September 1923. Emma passed away one month later.

The Ravensworth property was willed to their two sons, Henry and Carroll, who subsequently rented the house to Richard Baylor Hickman of Kentucky. Richard and his wife Stannye Ormsby purchased Ravensworth in 1926 and began renovations to the house a year later.

Ravensworth was soon to become the scene of an attempted assassination. One evening Richard Hickman was sitting in his library, quietly reading a book, when suddenly a bullet pierced the air and lodged itself into the panelling, three inches above his head. Hickman jumped to his feet and ran out of the house to search the grounds for his assailant. Unable to find the culprit, he retired for the night with the intention of notifying the police the next morning. During the night the assassin returned, entered the home, proceeded to the library, and removed the bullet from the wall. The assassin was never found.

Richard's wife, Stannye, died in 1936. He passed away in 1947.

Ravensworth was advertised for sale in the *Cobourg World* on Wednesday, December 3, 1947. The ad read, "$60,000 is being asked for the estate of 75 acres with 300 feet frontage on Lake Ontario, one and half miles east of Cobourg."

Ravensworth remained vacant until 1952, when it was purchased by John Weir Foote.

He was a Second World War veteran who was a recipient of the Victory Cross and who had been a Cabinet Minister under Lesley Frost. He owned the property from 1952 to 1963 when it was sold to Dr. and Mrs. D.E. Mikel. In 1973 it was purchased by Mr. And Mrs. J. Peters who were still the owners at the time of this writing.

THE MACKENZIE ESTATE, KIRKFIELD

The setting, architectural style, and interior trim of a house all reflect the owner's character. This was certainly true of Sir William Mackenzie, Canada's railroad baron, who built a stately brick house in Kirkfield, Ontario.

Mackenzie, the son of a Scottish immigrant born in 1849, began his railroad career with a contract to supply railway ties for the tracks to be laid in his area. In 1884, he received his first major contract, which involved the construction of a railway section in the Rocky Mountains for the Canadian Pacific Railway. While working on this project Mackenzie met Donald Mann, a subcontractor working on the next section of the CPR line through the Rockies. These two men shared a mutual bond of respect, and subsequently decided to combine their individual talents.

Their first railroad was a one-track line that went one hundred kilometres from Dauphin to Winnipegosis in Manitoba. This railroad allowed grain to be shipped from the southern prairies to grain vessels for distribution to larger populated centres. Next they decided to build a railroad across the northern prairies, using specialized equipment and methods that enabled them to lay a mile of track per day.

In 1877, Sir William built a forty-room mansion for his family. Lady Mackenzie was an avid gardener and often brought back exotic vegetation from Europe, to enhance their landscape. She had a wooden, water tower constructed close to the house, to provide an ample supply of water for her gardens; Sir William built a nine-hole golf course on the property.

This stately forty-room mansion was the home of Sir William Mackenzie, Canada's railroad baron.

Lady Mackenzie was extremely sensitive about the appearance of the village of Kirkfield, and if a building did not appear respectable, it was not unusual for a crew of men to be sent to paint the house, at her ladyship's expense, of course.

In 1911, William Mackenzie and Donald Mann were knighted by King George V. By that time their assets and holdings amounted to billions. A year later they decided to expand their northern railway coast to coast. They invested their fortune in this enormous project, but millions more dollars were needed. The Canadian government was reluctant to lend money to railroad barons, but finally agreed, with stringent conditions attached. The terms became too difficult for any man to meet, and the government foreclosed when the company defaulted on a payment in 1916. One year later, Mann and Mackenzie lost everything. The government took over operations and changed the name from Canadian Northern to Canadian National. At the time of his death in 1923, Sir William Mackenzie had little wealth.

His family sold the Mackenzie estate for one dollar, to the Sisters of St. Joseph. The house became a boarding school and later a retreat. In

1976, the Sisters sold the property to Mr. and Mrs. D. MacDonald-Ross. The Mackenzie house was turned into a museum to honour the life and times of Sir William Mackenzie. The coach house became a restaurant.

The MacDonald-Ross family worked tirelessly to maintain the Mackenzie estate and operate the restaurant. They had immigrated from Ireland, and were keenly aware of the importance of preserving history and heritage buildings. Sir William and Lady Mackenzie had played a vital role in the construction and preservation of buildings in the village of Kirkfield, and the MacDonald-Rosses would preserve the Mackenzie heritage.

Ultimately, it became too much financially for MacDonald-Rosses; they were forced to give up their dream, but it is thanks to them that the Mackenzie estate and legacy remain. Future owners have continued to operate the estate in different ways, from a bed and breakfast to catering weddings and housing workshops. There is no doubt that the majestic Mackenzie estate, after all these years, still reflects the vision of a man who wanted to connect a country from coast to coast by rail.

PERTH

The town of Perth got its name from the first capital of Scotland, and the Tay River was named for the Tay Estuary. They were so named in 1816 when Upper and Lower Canada were colonies.

During the previous fifty years, England had been fully occupied with war: Napoleon had been defeated at the battle of Waterloo; there had been the American and French revolutions; and there was the War of 1812 between the British and American forces. English states had turned their attention to colonization and the establishment of strategic out-posts, which would form defence lines back from the St. Lawrence River boundary and the United States.

Perth was the chief military settlement of these early schemes. This happened after the War of 1812, when officers and soldiers were given land grants in this area. They were, in effect, a trained reserve force. Farm implements and rations were free so that soldiers could survive through their first few years on the land.

Free passage from Britain, more free land, and a ten pound loan were offered, the loan to be repaid before the settler gained title to his land. Each family was given blankets, a saw, a hammer, chisels, nails, a grindstone, an auger, pot, and kettle, and one cross-cut saw to be shared by every four men.

The first group who acted on the offer and settled in Perth were low-landers, who left Glasgow in May 1815, aboard four transports. They wintered in Brockville, then thirty families travelled overland on foot to the area now known as Perth.

The town plot was laid out by June 1816. The Tay River was bridged and the clearing of the town site was begun. These early Scottish pioneer settlers were soon joined by more settlers from Ireland and Scotland.

By 1823, Perth contained a jail and courthouse, four churches, seven merchant stores, five taverns, and more than fifty wooden homes. The first store was established by William Morris, who was instrumental in promoting and constructing the first Tay Canal. The first brick buildings were the jail and the courthouse, in 1821–22.

The first stone house was built by a merchant in 1821, and from then on many houses and buildings were constructed of stone in the style that has remained characteristic of Perth to this day.

The completion of the Rideau Canal in 1832 gave Perth a direct line of communication as well as means of conveyance on the Ottawa River. The Tay River was dredged and locks were constructed. Trade was brisk and for a time a large amount of traffic was carried on using flat-bottomed boats. Goods from Montreal were brought in barges up the Rideau Canal via Ottawa and then up the Tay River to Perth. Steamers were commonly used after the 1830s.

Perth was linked to the railway system in the 1850s. The Brockville and Ottawa Railway was opened to traffic on February 7, 1859, when the first train arrived in Perth from Brockville. The journey in this train — a wood-burning locomotive and two coaches — took nine hours and forty minutes to cover fewer than forty miles.

Perth, today, has a country charm despite its more formal houses. The stone buildings lining the streets remain unchanged and tourists can sit by the river, sipping wine in a charming inn near the bridge. A romantic spot in a historical setting — you bet.

CORNWALL

The city of Cornwall is one of the oldest settlements in the province, having been founded around 1790 by refugees from the thirteen colonies. The exact date of the first families' arrival in the area is not known, but we do know that these early settlers welcomed United Empire Loyalists in 1784.

According to Nick and Helma Mika in their book entitled *Places in Ontario*, "This settlement was named New Johnstown after an older Johnstown in the Mohawk Valley, probably the former home of some of the settlers. In 1786, they received a large influx of highland Scots. In 1797, the name of the community was changed to Cornwall, apparently in honour of Prince George, who was the Duke of Cornwall, and the eldest son of King George the third."

The district courthouse and jail, located on the corner of Pitt and Water Streets, was completed in 1802. The two-storey frame structure was destroyed by fire in 1826. It was replaced by the present building in 1833 to serve as the courthouse and jail of the Eastern District. Today, the building is one of the province's oldest remaining public structures.

In 1834, Cornwall was incorporated as a town governed by an elected Board of Police, and became entitled to have representation in the Provincial House of Assembly. With incorporation, work began on a canal to enable shipping to bypass the Long Sault Rapids. The canal was opened for traffic in 1842. The construction of the canal brought a considerable influx of population to Cornwall and led to a change in the municipal government of the town. In 1846, the Board of Police was succeeded by a mayor and council.

The city's first policeman was Samuel Pollack, appointed in 1860 to maintain law and order. One of his prime duties was the lighting of the street lamps at dusk. A few years later the police force consisted of three officers.

The completion of the Grand Trunk Railway between Montreal and Toronto, in 1856, was welcomed by Cornwall and the surrounding area. Originally the railway line had been mapped to pass about five kilometres north of the town, and it took all the persuasive arguments that the town council and Cornwall's influential citizens could muster to get the route changed and bring it closer to the city. The combination of rail and water transportation placed Cornwall in a favourable position to attract diversified businesses and industries.

The Mikas added, "Cornwall's first permanent bank, the Bank of Montreal, was established in 1857. Service was initially provided in the store of William Mattice, who acted as agent. His store stood on what later became the site of the old post office building; a landmark for many years before it was demolished to make way for the St. Lawrence Seaway Authority's projects.

"Streetcars first appeared on Cornwall's streets in 1896. The original Cornwall Street Railway Company was reorganized in 1902 as the Cornwall Railway, Light and Power Company Limited. In the early days of the street railway, the company possessed three open cars which travelled between Water Street and what is now the Canadian National Railways Station."

Older residents can recall a public library that was located at that time in a section of a hardware store, a building that has since disappeared.

The seven-storey Seaway Authority Headquarters building opened in 1957, and is one of the city's main tourist attractions. Another seaway-related attraction is the Robert H. Saunders St. Lawrence Generating Station, which is visited yearly by 100,000 people. Begun in 1954 and completed four years later, the hydro-electric station generates power for Eastern Ontario. It was named for a former chairman of Ontario Hydro and the power station comprises three dams and sixteen miles of dikes.

BROOKLIN

The first funeral to take place in Brooklin was the burial of the undertaker's wife, Nancy Holt.

The community of Brooklin, located just north of Whitby, was originally called Winchester. The first clearing made for a log shanty was on the north side of the Sixth Concession, east of Brooklin.

In 1840, there were four log houses in the settlement occupied by John McGee, Amos Way, the Campbell family, and William Hepenstal. It was John and Robert Campbell who built a flour mill on the banks of a stream known as Bickell's Creek. A short time later they added a grist and a sawmill to their enterprises. Around these mills grew a settlement. At one time seven mills were operated within a distance of five kilometres on Bickell's Creek.

By 1846, there were three hundred residents. There was a doctor — Dr. Alliston — one grist mill, one ashery, one tannery, seven stores, three taverns, two wagon makers, three blacksmiths and one cabinetmaker. That same year, through the persistence of Peter Perry, the government assumed the responsibility of a new road. This road was the first plank construction and extended from Port Whitby to Port Perry. The planks, which were of the finest pine, were four inches thick and fourteen feet long, and laid diagonally.

By 1850, Brooklin had about 550 residents and was becoming a major manufacturing centre. There were several mills, a tannery, a potashery, a foundry, a woollen factory, a brewery, two baking soda factories, and a soap and candle factory.

A circulating library was in operation at this time, and shortly thereafter Brooklin organized their first fall fair. In 1868 Brooklin was host to the Dominion Plowing Match. Randy Miller, a real estate agent, described some of the downtown buildings. "Among the early downtown buildings there is an old hotel built in 1883, and now used as the Royal Canadian Legion. A three-storey yellow brick store was once the Whitby Township Hall. Brooklin was a milling centre for grinding wheat into flour. Near the downtown, on Cassels Road, there is one of the oldest brick flour mills in Ontario. Built in 1848, it was fully operational until 1989. The building has accommodated retail and service business since that time and remains very much the same as it was."

Stephen Mede Thomas arrived in Brooklin in the late 1850s with his four brothers. Four years later he purchased land and began construction of his house. It was a grand edifice, one of Brooklin's largest residences with a row of cedars planted on either side of the walkway leading to the house. Stephen named his new home Cedar Cliff. It sat on a small knoll with a creek meandering beside it, and overlooked the main street. Shortly after its completion he built a two-storey brick general store north of the creek on the west side, immediately south of the house.

In 1872, Thomas turned ten acres of land on the Fifth Concession into Graveside Cemetery, with plots laid out and ready for use by the spring of 1874.

By 1881, Stephen Thomas had sold Cedar Cliff to Richard Moore for thirty-five hundred dollars and moved to the United States. Cedar Cliff changed ownership nine times until James and Wilma Carnwith purchased it in 1948 for $23,000. The Carnwith family took great pride in Cedar Cliff and the house continued to be surrounded by beautiful gardens. Although the Carnwith family eventually sold Cedar Cliff, it still remains standing as a reminder to Brooklin and its unique history.

Today, Brooklin is rapidly colliding with Oshawa and Whitby, but its old town centre is still unique and quaint.

SCUGOG ISLAND

Scugog Island, adjacent to Port Perry, is sixteen kilometres long and four wide, approximately eleven thousand acres of land.

The name Scugog is a First Nations word meaning submerged or flooded land. That name came from Peter Jones, an Ojibwa missionary who worked among the Mississauga First Nations on the island in the 1800s. It is a derivation of Wuh-yoy-wus-ki-wuh-gog, shallow muddy lake.

The island was first surveyed in 1816 by Major S. Wilmot, and at that time a number of Mississaugas inhabited the island and vicinity. A paper presented to the Canadian Institute on January 12, 1889, by A.F. Chamberlain, however, indicates earlier habitation of the island by the Mohawks (Iroquois).

The first recorded white settler on the island was Joseph Graxton in 1834. On November 3, 1843, the Mississaugas of Lake Scugog purchased eight hundred acres of land on the island. It became known as the Scugog Indian Reserve. The government hired William Taylor to build twelve houses and three barns. This was the government's attempt to induce Aboriginal peoples to live as white men. Some farm machinery was also supplied. None of these efforts altered the Mississaugas' chosen living style.

In 1847, the missionary report indicated a population of sixty-four people. In 1866, the band numbered thirty-eight people, even though eight hundred inhabitants were recorded living on the island.

It was no easy task to settle and clear the island for cattle. Animals had to be transported from the mainland to the island, which meant that the first thing to be done was to build a ferry or scow.

Many tragic stories have been told of the old ferry powered by two men with oars and of the isolation of living in wild lands. One story tells of John Thompson, George Gilbert, and Gilbert's seventeen-year-old son who started out on the ferry from Paxton's Point to the island. The lake was rougher than they expected, and the animals on board, frightened, began to stir. This included a team of horses and a yoke of oxen. Young Gilbert attempted to hold them, but was carried overboard in the confusion.

George Gilbert jumped in to save his son, but both of them drowned.

Fishing on Lake Scugog has also provided people with stories. There was a time when you could fill a boat with fish in no time. No record was kept of the biggest fish in these waters, but one man stuck his spear into what he supposed was a log at the bottom of the lake and it turned out to be a muskellunge that tipped the scales at fifty pounds.

In 1857, and again in 1904, great numbers of fish were killed. The lake level was low, the waters were exceptionally severe, and the water froze almost to the bottom. There were no air holes and many fish died as a result. When people cut holes to fish in the winter, the holes were swarmed by fish in need of air. People filled as many bags as they could carry. That spring paid witness to masses of dead fish.

The island today is no longer an island because a causeway connects it to the mainland, a causeway often lined with fishing tourists.

Scugog Island is still a farming community and it also has a good museum which pays tribute to the early pioneers and the Aboriginal peoples. In the 1900s there were very good Aboriginal basketmakers on Scugog Island. It even has a casino, several subdivisions, a heron colony, a famous ghost, and a Buddhist community.

STIRLING

The quaint village of Stirling, nestled in the picturesque hills and valleys of Hastings County, was first settled in 1797. John Bleecker and Caleb Gilbert of Sidney Township were allotted a mill site there on Rawdon Creek. Bleecker died before the completion of the mill. The mill was eventually completed by Samuel Rosebush in 1807.

Several Aboriginal burial grounds were discovered in the surrounding area of Stirling in the early days. Mr. George Bailey, a barber for many years in the settlement, was said to have an amazing collection of Aboriginal artifacts, unsurpassed by many museums.

Among the earliest settlers were Edward Fidlar, who came from the Orkney Islands (a group of more than seventy islands off the northeast tip of Scotland), and Robert Parker, who came from Ayr, near Stirlingshire, Scotland, in 1821. Parker came as a secretary-treasurer for the family interest in the nearby Marmora Mines. When the mines proved unsuccessful, he eventually settled in Stirling, where he operated a tavern. Fidlar had gone into the mill business, and together these men helped to shape the growth and development of Stirling.

The hamlet was known by many names: sometimes called Fidlar's Mills, at other times the settlement was called Sheldon Mills for mill owner Sheldon Hawley, and sometimes it was called Rawdon Mills for the township. Since many of the early pioneers had Scottish roots and the surrounding countryside reminded them of Stirlingshire in their homeland, Stirling was the name that ultimately prevailed.

Roads and industries got under way. The nearest place where groceries could be purchased was Kingston. A comic story is told of a husband who had been away for two weeks to get a piece of glass for their broken window, and when he arrived back home they were so happy to be together again that they accidentally broke the glass when they embraced.

Maple sugar was the only sweetener for tea and coffee. Coffee was made from dried and partially charred peas and barley or hemlock. Footwear was a luxury and worn only when it was necessary.

In the 1850s, a visitor described the settlement as "a very pretty, rural place ... fast rising towards the dignity of a town." Rawdon's township hall had been built in Stirling in 1850. In 1858, Stirling was incorporated as a village. During this time the area became a market centre, with a population nearing 1,000. There was a large flour mill, a woollen factory, a sash and blind factory and shops and stores of every description.

The milling of timber was the first industry in this area. The land on which Stirling was built was among the first to provide huge trees for the shipbuilding industries of England, Scotland, and Europe.

According to the publication *The Heritage Years: A History of Stirling and District*, "In the decades that followed incorporation a slow, but already steady, growth continued. As travel became easier, the need for many small industries to produce locally diminished, and it was possible to have goods brought in from larger centres. However, it continued to be a centre for trade and services, and several hotels provided accommodation as they came to market. One was the Mansion House, later renamed the Kerby House and then the Paisley House. In what is now called the Empire Block, was the Scott House, later called the Moon Hotel. Just east was the Exchange Hotel, and another was operated by George Whitty, and became known as the Stirling House."

Like so many other early settlements, fire was the cause of incredible destruction. The Exchange Hotel was destroyed in a fire on June 14, 1883, which had spread through a large part of the business district. Another fire struck on August 9, 1908, and it also destroyed many business establishments.

Flooding was yet another cause of destruction in the community. The flood of 1980 had many people recalling floods of 1959, 1936, and of 1928.

Despite the fires and flooding, Stirling remains a viable centre of activity.

NIAGARA FALLS

Niagara Falls is the greatest waterfall, by volume, in the world. Split in two by a land ridge, the American Falls are sixty-four metres high and 305 metres wide, with a flow of fourteen million litres of water per minute. The Canadian Horseshoe Falls are fifty-four metres high and 675 metres wide, with a flow of 155 million litres per minute. The falls were formed only 10,000 years ago as retreating glaciers exposed the Niagara Escarpment, and diverted the waters of Lake Erie, which had previously drained into Lake Ontario. The falls have eroded the soft shale and limestone of the escarpment by 1.2 metres per year and now stand eleven kilometres from their place of origin at present-day Queenston.

The existence of the falls was well known prior to the arrival of missionary Father Hennepin. The Aboriginal peoples had directed early explorers there to see these magnificent waters of the Earth Mother, and the origin of the name Niagara, although disputed by some, is probably of Aboriginal origin, a word meaning "thundering of water."

On Monday June 30, 1792, Mrs. John Graves Simcoe recorded her visit to the falls in her diary. She wrote, "After an excellent breakfast we ascended an exceedingly steep road to the top of the mountain which commands a fine view of the country as far as the garrison of Niagara and across the lake. From hence the road is entirely flat to the falls, of which I did not hear the sound until within a mile of them. The falls is said to be but 170 feet in height. The river previously rushed in the most rapid manner on a declivity for three miles, and those rapids are a fine sight."

In *The Diary of Elizabeth Simcoe*, edited by John Ross Robertson, Mrs. Simcoe describes her venture at Niagara Falls.

> I descended an exceedingly steep hill to go to the Table Rock, from whence the view of the falls is tremendously fine. After taking some refreshments on Table Rock, we went three miles to Chippawa Fort, admiring the rapids all the way. People cross from Chippawa to Fort Schlosser, but great caution is necessary, the current is so extremely strong, and if they did not make exactly the mouth of the Chippawa the force of the water below it would inevitably carry them down the falls without redress. Eight soldiers, who were intoxicated, met with this accident in crossing the river some years since. An Indian was asleep in his canoe near Fort Schlosser. The canoe was tied to a tree; some person cut the rope; he did not wake until the canoe had got into the strong current. He found all his endeavours to paddle ineffectual, and was seen to lay himself down, resigning himself to this fate, and was soon carried down the falls.

The first white settlers to locate near the falls were United Empire Loyalists. By 1790, the region was well populated, although settlement remained quite scattered. The construction of the first suspension bridge across the Niagara River in 1848 assisted settlement nearer to the falls.

By 1846, The Maid of the Mist steamboats began sailing passengers to the base of the cataracts. The steamboat's name is derived from a legend about a beautiful Aboriginal maid who, because of an unhappy love triangle, plunged to her death over the falls.

Tourism has always been a major industry for Niagara Falls, even back to Confederation when 150,000 tourists flocked to the falls on a yearly basis. Never missing an opportunity to make money, the hucksters arrived there in 1825. They occupied a mile-long stretch of the Niagara riverbank, which became known as The Front. Many local residents disapproved of The Front and felt it was a stain on the landscape that should be removed. In 1878, they managed to exert enough pressure on the government to force expropriation and push the unscrupulous hucksters out. The shoddiness was then replaced by parklands enjoyed today by one and all.

Niagara Falls is the home of myriad tourist enjoyments, such as Louis Tussaud's Waxworks, Ripley's Believe It or Not, the Botanical Gardens, and Marineland, with its famous entranceway designed by Ontario's own Bill Lishman. Its proximity to the fruit belt and Niagara-on-the-Lake, with its rich history, makes a trip there memorable.

Courtesy of the Ontario Archives.

A family poses for a portrait with Niagara Falls in the background. Around 1867, approximately 150,000 tourists flocked to the falls on a yearly basis.

PENMARVIAN, PARIS

In 1674, in Chester, England, fourteen-year-old Banfield Capron stowed away aboard a New England-bound vessel. He landed on the coast near Rhode Island and within six years he had purchased, cleared, and cultivated a large tract of land. When he was thirty-four, life had become too routine and civilized for him, so he trekked farther inland to the Massachusetts frontier, where he spent the remainder of his years farming. He raised twelve children.

Several generations later, the restless and determined spirit of Banfield Capron surfaced again in Hiram Capron, who left home at the age of twenty to seek his fortune. He began his career as a bookkeeper for a blast furnace business near the settlement of Rochester, New York. Six years later he was the principal partner in a foundry that he had established himself, on the Canadian shore of Lake Erie near Normandale, Ontario.

During his travels for the foundry he discovered a tract of land near the forks where the Nith River tumbled into the fast-flowing Grand. The land, thickly covered with pine and oak, sloped sharply upwards to a level, oak plain and beyond to the rolling hills around Galt. This scene reminded him of the youth he had spent hunting and fishing in the Green Mountains of New York. He pictured the land for farming and the water power harnessed for mills and industry.

Hiram purchased the land in 1829, and moved his young family to the new area. He successfully raised enough money to improve Governor's

Road (surveyed and built in 1793) and to build a bridge across the Grand River. Settlers were soon to come.

The two rivers provided remarkable natural advantages for manufacturing with an abundance of water power. The town was named Paris because of the extensive gypsum beds found on the south bank of the Nith River.

His land was surveyed into streets and lots and the lots were offered free to settlers. A dam was built with raceways and grinding mills. This brought many enterprising business people and hardworking settlers to the new village of Paris. The villagers called Capron "King."

The house he built was made of square-hewn stone in a simplified classical revival design; it crowned the hill overlooking Paris, commanding his favourite view of the Grand River below as it wound south to the wooded banks at the forks. The house was large enough to accommodate his family of six children, but was still sedate and restrained.

Many cobblestone houses were built from the river-bottoms, making Paris the cobblestone capital of Ontario.

The second owner of Hiram Capron's house was John Penman of the Paris textile mills. He gave it the name "Penmarvian." These were Victorian times, and Penman attempted to transform the house into a castle with a conical tower, fancy gables, and blocky, pink columns. The home was willed, in 1939, to the Presbyterian church, and it was used as a retirement home for ministers. In the 1960s and '70s it was made available for rent as a family home, an attempt to prevent it from reaching abandoned status. In 1977, the owner of a construction firm bought Penmarvian and began extensive renovations to restore it.

The original beauty of King Capron's home died with him in 1872, and although his six children left no descendants, their names remain alive as street names in Paris: Emily, William, Mary, Banfield, Jane, and Charlotte.

WASAGA BEACH

Wasaga Beach, once known as Schooner Town and as a naval establishment on Lake Huron, played an important role in the War of 1812. It was here that the schooner *Nancy*, built in 1789, saw military service during the war. The ship was used to carry supplies north to Fort Michilimackinac and on one of these trips the *Nancy* was pursued two miles up the Nottawasaga River by three American vessels. Lieutenant Worsley, who was in command, refused to admit defeat, although the odds were overwhelmingly against him. The *Nancy* had only three guns and a crew of twenty-three, compared to the twenty-four guns and five hundred crewmen on the American vessels. Despite the odds, Worsley turned to fight the enemy, who quickly sank the *Nancy*, but not before the lieutenant and his crew succeeded in departing the ship and in securing their supplies in the bush. Shortly thereafter reinforcements arrived from St. Joseph's and Worsley struck out against the enemy once more. This time he seized two of the American schooners.

An accumulation of silt over the years has covered the sunken hull of the *Nancy* and in time has created an island by the same name. This island today supports a museum commemorating those early days, a lighthouse, and a theatre.

At the entrance of Nancy Island there is an historic plaque dedicated to the first manned flight from the mainland of Canada to England. It was from Wasaga Beach, on the morning of August 8, 1934, that James R. Ayling and Leonard G. Reid took off in their plane, *The Trail of the*

Caribou, bound for Baghdad. Adverse weather conditions and a shortage of fuel forced them to land at Heston Airfield in London, England, on the afternoon of August 9th; they flew 6,000 kilometres in thirty hours and fifty-five minutes.

Wasaga Beach itself features a magnificent strip of fine, sandy beach curving in an eleven-kilometre-long crescent around the southeastern corner of Nottawasaga Bay, and extends inland along the Nottawasaga River. In the background, Blue Mountain towers over three hundred metres above the water.

Before the turn of the century, nearby residents frequented Wasaga Beach by horse and buggy to picnic and to swim. By 1925, there were hundreds of cottages on the beach, four thousand cars, and fifteen thousand people on any given sunny, summer Sunday. Two years later those figures, on a holiday weekend, increased to forty thousand visitors.

During the Second World War, Canada's large military base, Camp Borden located nearby, drew soldiers to the beach, its dance halls, and to tourist cabins for weekend recreation. Crowds were often estimated as high as 100,000 on a weekend during the war, and were even larger after the declaration of peace.

Weekend traffic continued to increase into the 1950s. More and more hotels opened up around Wasaga Beach. The demand for cottages increased and real estate developers bought up miles of lake-front property and divided it into small lots. The endless stretches of over-crowded shoreline began to resemble suburban streets.

Post-war prosperity saw improved highways and faster cars on the road. Residents of Toronto and other metropolitan centres began to feel the need to get out into the country. The increased affluence and shorter workweeks gave way to more leisure and the indulgence of country retreats.

Today there are several miles of innumerable, garishly decorated emporiums, bowling alleys, tourist cabins, motels, taverns, arcades, and restaurants. Some people say it is Coney Island, Atlantic City, and Toronto's old Sunnyside all rolled into one.

Wasaga Beach works to maintain a balance in what the environment can handle in terms of people. In 1962, the Ministry of Natural

Resources and Forestry limited access to the beach area to four controlled entrances. There are no schooners to contend with, but there still is the military and an ever-increasing number of tourists.

KINCARDINE

The year was 1848. Two men, Allan Cameron and William Withers, embarked from a schooner and set up camp on the beach near the river. They called this place Pentangore, a corruption of the Indian name Na-Benem-tan-gauh, meaning "the river with the sand on one side." Today it is called Kincardine in honour of James Bruce, Earl of Elgin and Kincardine, Governor General of Canada, 1847–1854.

Withers and Cameron erected a log house, which Mr. Cameron opened as a hotel. A few pioneers joined them that summer and a settlement was started on the flats by the present-day harbour and beach.

The need for a gristmill was keenly felt by these settlers, who raised the first harvests of grain in the County of Bruce. William Sutton constructed a dam across the north branch of the Penetangore River and built a mill at what is now known as Sutton's Hollow.

It wasn't until 1856 that the market square was logged and burned. Princess Street was cleared, but a good sugar bush still flourished where South Street is today. Where the water tower now stands there were giant hemlocks. The river, instead of flowing straight out into the lake as it does now, wound through town with a sharp bend to the south, and then ran parallel to the beach for about three hundred yards. This meandering course meant many bridges in the town.

A harbour was established in 1855, and a breakwater was constructed of timber cribs and filled with stone. The power of the storms on Lake Huron had been underestimated and the breakwater was washed

The harbour of Kincardine was established in 1855. The lighthouse served to guide the fishing fleets home at night.

away in only a few months. The following year work commenced on the construction of two parallel piers thirty metres apart at the mouth of the river. The pier on the north side was 165 metres long and the one on the south side was fifty-eight metres long. They still stand today.

A fishing industry was started in Kincardine in the 1850s, and by 1966, six boats sailed each morning from the harbour to lift and set their nets. Fish were plentiful and sizeable in Lake Huron at that time. In July of 1875, Samuel Splan caught a salmon-trout weighing thirty-four kilograms. The fishing industry flourished until lamprey eels interfered with the trout population of Lake Huron.

Large deposits of salt were discovered in 1868, and the Kincardine Salt Prospecting and Manufacturing Company was formed. The first salt well was 320 metres down and located north of the harbour. The second well was located south of the harbour. The separation process involved wood-fired boilers that were very costly to run, and the company closed after a very short time.

In the 1870s the Wellington Grey and Bruce Railway built an extension northward to Kincardine, from Palmerston. In 1875, Kincardine was incorporated into a town.

Kincardine has a distinct Scottish community that faithfully celebrates Robbie Burns Day, piping in the haggis for a midnight feast after an evening of fun and dance.

When Ontario Hydro built the Bruce Nuclear Power Station at Douglas Point in the 1970s, there was a considerable economic impact on the town. Employment opportunities were abundant and business increased to meet the needs of the larger community. A large hydroponic greenhouse business emerged as a by-product of the nuclear plant. Thousands of gallons of heated water have been rerouted to supply this new enterprise.

Kincardine is, in 2016, still a very viable town and some impressive condominium developments have emerged that have views of the lake. The beaches continue to be long and beautiful from there north to Southampton and south to Grand Bend and beyond.

ELORA

The first white settler to arrive in what is now Elora was Roswell Mathews, a Welshman from the United States. He arrived here in 1817. He was contracted as a carpenter and millwright to build a dam and sawmill for James Crooks, the agent for General Pilington. They chose a site by the falls but were unable to secure a firm footing and the dam washed out in the spring floods. Forced to find a market, General Pilington and his sons hollowed out a pine log nine metres long to make a dugout canoe. This, they launched two kilometres below the falls, loaded it with sixteen bags of wheat, and paddled down to Galt. There he sold his wheat for fifty cents a bushel and the dugout was sold for $2.50. They returned on foot.

The washout occurred every year for several years until, discouraged, he left the area.

The area languished then, until the arrival of Captain Gilkinson in 1832. Gilkinson, a cousin of John Galt, founder of the city of Guelph, was a native of Irvine, Scotland. He planned a new settlement at the junction of the Grand and Irvine Rivers, near another set of falls. He was recently retired from lake service with the North West Company, and gladly purchased 14,000 acres of land at a reported $2.50 an acre. He named this new village Elora as the caves near the falls reminded him of the famous Elora Temple in India.

Before his untimely death the next year, Gilkinson had established a sawmill and a general store in Elora. Soon the hamlet boasted a tavern and a blacksmith, while a post office was opened in 1839.

Courtesy of the Ontario Archives.

A church outing at the Elora Gorge.

Author's Collection.

The stone work remains standing despite the loss of the building.

The house of Mr. Thomas McManus on Walnut Street was once known as Martin's Tavern. Early stories say that the tavern was haunted. These stories arose, no doubt, from talks of a murder that was committed there.

The first business street was Victoria Street, with three new stores in 1852, but it was along Mill Street and Lower Metcalfe Streets that the first real business centre began to be developed in the 1860s.

In 1857, several Aboriginal peoples, from the shores of the Upper Lakes, visited Elora in search of the treasure that their forefathers had hidden among the "rocks by the singing waters." They left without discovering anything. Little did they know that just a few yards from a place the settlers called "the hole-in-the-rock" there was a cave in the face of the cliff in the Elora Gorge. There in that cave, two hundred years earlier, the Neutral Indians had hidden their precious wampum beads. It wasn't until a Sunday afternoon in 1880 that two boys, Foxy Hillis and Corky MacDonald, found several of the wampum beads, which had been washed from the cave by an unusually heavy rain. When the boys showed their teacher, David Boyle, he carefully sifted the fine earth from the cave and secured the treasure that the Aboriginal peoples had failed to find. Some of those beads are in the Royal Ontario Museum in Toronto.

Elora today is still very beautiful and peaceful despite an influx of tourism. Many stone structures and old architecture remain and the gorge itself is still gorgeous.

THE CONANT HOMESTEAD, OSHAWA

On October 15, 1792, Roger Conant landed on Canadian soil at Newark (now Niagara-on-the-Lake) having crossed the Niagara River on a flat-bottomed scow ferry. He journeyed eastward along the north shore of Lake Ontario until he arrived in Darlington, and there he hastily built a log dwelling before winter set in.

After he had blazed some eight hundred acres, Roger chose to become a fur trader with the Aboriginal peoples. Once he had amassed a small fortune, he left his spacious and comfortable log cabin in 1811 and built a frame home near the Oshawa harbour. Roger had no way of knowing that his new home would play a part in the War of 1812.

When General Hull surrendered his whole command of two thousand, five hundred men at Detroit, on August 15, 1812, a serious question arose. What would the British do with so many prisoners?

The redcoats decided to send the American prisoners to Quebec. Due to an insufficient numbers of boats, many men were compelled to walk along the shore of Lake Ontario. The prisoners and guards were offered food at various places along the route. When they arrived at Roger Conant's house without warning, the family quickly set a large pot of potatoes on the fire to boil. Fortunately a churning of butter had been done that day and a ham had been boiled the preceding day. The guards were outnumbered two to one, but no one escaped while feasting at this home.

A few days before Roger Conant died in 1821, he buried his gold in a large iron kettle on the bank of Salmon Creek. When the kettle was missed from its accustomed position by the open fireplace, a search began but failed to reveal its whereabouts. Many have attempted to recover this buried treasure, but all have failed.

During the uprising of 1837–38, the Upper Canada Rebellion, Roger's son Daniel and his family resided in the house. On a winter's night of 1837, at midnight, Colonel Ferguson arrived at the Conant home and had his men surround the residence. The Conants were turned out into the snow while their house was ransacked and searched. Those were gloomy days for men whose lives and liberties were unsafe in Canada.

The Conant homestead was also the birthplace of Thomas Conant, one of Canada's famous writers and author of *Upper Canada Sketches and Life in Canada.*

The homestead remained in the Conant family until it was sold to the city of Oshawa in 1959. Prior to this, Mrs. Verna Conant wished to move the house down to the park by the lake among Oshawa's other historic buildings, but her wish was never granted by the city.

The house could not be saved and the land was required for future development. In 1959, the Oshawa fire department arrived at the homestead and burned the building to the ground.

Today, few buildings of stylish architecture and historical significance remain standing in Oshawa. The land where the Conant house once stood still remains vacant, leaving all to wonder about future development.

It was my pleasure to meet Verna Conant when she was in her nineties. We sat by the fireplace warming ourselves on a cold winter night. Mrs. Conant talked to me about her incredible life and her involvement over the years with the Girl Guides of Canada. At one point she ushered me into a room containing bookshelves of personal journals that she had written since childhood. It was truly a memorable evening. Mrs. Conant died the following year.

MOOSE FACTORY AND MOOSONEE

In 1673, the Company of Adventurers of England, known as the Hudson's Bay Company, established Moose Factory, the first English-speaking community in Upper Canada. The post known as Moose Fort was built on Moose Island by Governor Charles Bayly.

Moose Factory was the second trading post to be established in the area. Moosonee, located across the water, had been the site of a trading post operated by the Revillon Frères trading company. The French called the post Moosonee, which was named after the Cree word *Moosonee*, "at the Moose." This site was Ontario's only saltwater port.

In 1686, a French expedition from Montreal captured Moose Fort from the English trading company and renamed it St Louis. It was later restored to Britain, but was not reopened until 1730. A fire destroyed the post in 1735, and it was rebuilt to serve as the Hudson's Bay Company's principal post in the James Bay Region. In 1850, an Anglican mission was established here.

This area of land is known as the Hudson Bay Lowlands, also known as the Hudson Platform, and was covered by glaciers ten thousand years ago. Aboriginal peoples occupied the area on a seasonal basis. Anthropologists identified the Aboriginal people as Swampy Cree. They lived in the seven coastal communities on James and Hudson Bay. The seasonal occupation may have been a result of game and fur-bearing animals not being numerous and food being in short supply. The district was visited twice a year by the Swampy Cree to hunt geese during the spring and autumn migrations. The Swampy Cree were hunters and fish-ermen, and their summer encampments were situated at the mouths of major rivers and usually contained about one hundred people. In the fall they dispersed into smaller groups.

The belief system of the Swampy Cree was well developed and it was strongly connected to the search for food. The first spring goose killed had a special significance. The head of that goose was dried, decorated with beads, and saved to honour the goose spirit. There was a ritual done when hunters needed to determine where to go for game. The rit-ual involved an elder holding the shoulder blade of a caribou over hot coals and then reading the cracked and burned spots that appeared in the bone. He would then know where to hunt for game.

In 1668, the renowned Medard Chouart, Sieur de Groseilliers, wintered at Fort Charles, later called Rupert House. That spring, three hundred Aboriginal people arrived to trade. Groseilliers returned to England in 1669, with great tales of a successful fur-trading expedition. A year later, a royal charter was granted to the "Governor and Company of Adventurers of England trading into Hudson Bay" and that marked the establishment of the Hudson's Bay Company.

That same year the company established trading posts. The first post was situated at the mouth of the Nelson River in 1670, the Moose River in 1673, the Albany River in 1683, and the Severn River in 1685. The presence of trading posts such as Moose Factory represented a radical departure from the Cree's mobile adaption to the environment of the lowland. The company depended on the Cree to deliver moose and caribou meat and geese when they came to the posts to trade. Gradually significant numbers of Cree came to live in the lowland all year round. The Cree soon became quite dependent on the trading posts for arms and ammunition as well as other items such as knives, hatchets, ice chisels, and clothing. These Cree who lived near the trading posts came to be known as the "Home Guard Cree" and they were the primary supplier of country food.

The Hudson's Bay Company's monopoly was challenged on a num-ber of occasions by French traders. The North West Company based in Montreal was operating trading posts north of Lake Superior and Lake Huron after the late 1760s. In 1821, a merger took place between the

Hudson's Bay Company and the North West Company. It handed its control over to the new Canadian government in 1870.

Moose Factory was the administrative centre for the company's James Bay district. During the early years of the twentieth century, Revillion Frères established trading posts throughout the James Bay area. In 1936, it was purchased by the Hudson's Bay Company.

In 1905, the Swampy Cree signed Treaty No. 9, with the province of Ontario and the Dominion of Canada, and adhesions to that treaty in 1929. This treaty ceded the land in the province of Ontario, north of the Albany River, and formalized the relationship between the Aboriginal peoples and the Federal Department of Indian Affairs. Reserves were established and residential schools were operated at Fort Albany (Roman Catholic) and Moose Factory (Anglican). At the time, several Métis families at Moose Factory and Fort Albany were included in Treaty No. 9, while other Métis families were apparently excluded from that same treaty.

The Hudson Bay Lowlands serves as a major migratory staging, breeding, and molting area for many of the Arctic and subarctic geese of eastern Canada. At various times of the year, an estimated four million geese and ducks occupy the Hudson Bay Lowlands.

The Aboriginal harvest shows great variation by season and by years. The size of the kill is dependent on the supply of geese, the number of hunters, and the weather. The use of firearms has allowed for the average waterfowl harvest per Aboriginal hunter to exceed one hundred birds a year. Non-Aboriginal residents of Moosonee and Moose Factory harvested more than five thousand birds in the fall of 1982, approximately thirteen birds per hunter. In 1982–83, the waterfowl harvest by Aboriginal hunters for the coastal villages of James Bay and Hudson Bay amounted to 36,197 birds during the spring hunt and 48,287 birds in the fall.

The Temiskaming and Northern Ontario Railway, now the Ontario Northland Railway, reached Moosonee on July 15, 1931. This vital link of transportation helped to connect the north with Cochrane, Ontario, and other parts further south.

Every year thousands of tourists make the trek north to Cochrane, and hop on board the Polar Bear Express to travel three hundred kilometres to the communities of Moose Factory and Moosonee. In the period from 1975 to 1983, there was on average 21,368 travellers per year.

At Moosonee you can visit the Revillon Frères Museum, see the marvelous artifacts from the French Company, and browse the craft stores. You also may want to take a trip on a large freighter canoe up the Moose River to search for Devonian fossils. The Wilderness Excursion, which is a six-hour trip that combines a cruise to James Bay and the Ship Sands Island Bird Sanctuary, might catch your fancy, too.

From Moosonee, you can take a boat to Moose Factory Island and see the original site of the Hudson's Bay post. Several early nineteenth century buildings remain, including a blacksmith's shop from 1740 and a museum devoted to the fur trade. You can also visit the Cree community situated on the island or stop in at St. Thomas Anglican Church with its Cree-language prayer books.

On my first trip to Cochrane, before boarding a train bound for Moosonee a few years ago, the first thing I saw at the Cochrane station was a coffin sitting out front. I felt, in that moment, that I had reached the last frontier and would definitely experience something new.

GORES LANDING

The physical geography of Gores Landing as it is today, on the shores of Rice Lake, began when the Wisconsin glacier receded twelve thousand years ago. The melt-water lakes, including the Kawarthas, were formed to the south. Rice Lake is commonly included in the chain of Kawartha Lakes, but, geologically, it is separate. The origin of the lake is pre-glacial.

The first people known to inhabit the Rice Lake area were the Palaeo Aboriginals. They were hunters of the caribou. Spear points found in the area are thought to date back 11,500 years ago. In the 1980s the heel bone of a woodland caribou was uncovered by Derek McBride while excavating for an addition to his cottage near Webb's Bay, situated on the south shore of Rice Lake.

There is a story around the crevice in a large granite stone at Sager Point, east of Harwood. Aboriginal peoples were said to have sharpened their tools there. It is considered to be an Aboriginal rubbing stone.

In the beginning of the eighteenth century, the Mississaugas, a branch of the Ojibwa, arrived and settled on the shores of Rice Lake. According to Norma Martin, Catherine Milne, and Donna McGillis in their book entitled *Gore's Landing and the Rice Lake Plains,*

> Tradition says that the Aboriginal peoples regarded Rice Lake as a sacred place and brought their aged chiefs and wounded warriors to its shore to be purified. It was this tribe of indigenous people who initiated the tradition of

Courtesy of the Ontario Archives

Ojibwa guide Billy Hogan and family on Rice Lake.

burning off the vegetation on the Rice Lake Plains located on the south shore. This practice encouraged the growth of a course grass relished by the deer and gave rise to their name for Rice Lake, *Pem-e-dash-cou-tay-ang*, "Lake of the Burning Plains." The French had earlier named the lake Folle Avoine, meaning Lake of Wild Oats.

In 1793, a trading post was established at the mouth of the Otonabee River on the north shore of Rice Lake. By the last quarter of the eighteenth century, most of the important fur-bearing animals were trapped-out (depleted by over-trapping) along the north shore of Lake Ontario. It was a challenging time for the Aboriginal peoples living in the area. According to the Reverend John MacLean in his book, *Vanguards of Canada, 1918*, the Mississaugas at Rice Lake were victims of alcohol provided by unscrupulous traders in Port Hope and Peterborough.

In the early 1800s wild rice became an important food for the Rice Lake Aboriginals. In 1817, it was reported that the rice in this lake grew so thickly that up to ten thousand bushels per year were harvested. Sadly, the wild rice beds have disappeared as result of a number of factors, including the change in lake levels following the construction of dams for the Trent Canal. The creation of the Trent system raised water levels on many lakes. In July 1928, a hurricane wreaked further havoc and, in 1950, the introduction of bottom-feeding carp was the last straw for most of the roots of the remaining rice plants.

In the 1840s, a settlement was begun on the south shore of the lake. The settlers called their home Gores Landing, named after Thomas S. Gore, a British Naval captain who had owned land here in 1845.

Gores Landing began to prosper when it became the terminal point of the plank road from Cobourg to Rice Lake in 1847. A stagecoach connection offered residents and visitors the opportunity to travel. A private boarding school, F.W. Barron Boy's School, was opened by a former headmaster of Upper Canada College. A hotel, a tavern, a general store, and several small industries made up the business section. In the early 1900s Gores Landing was a boatbuilding centre and a port of call for Rice Lake steamers.

In 1902, Canadian artist Gerald Sinclair Hayward built his summer home on the southern shores of Rice Lake. He called his home "The Willows." Today the structure is called Victoria Inn and is operated as a resort. The tower room in the building is a special one, as my wife and I can confirm.

The Aboriginal peoples went to Rice Lake for purification and that was our experience as well. It was a wild night of rain and lightning and one could open the tower windows in three of the four directions (and we did). The power of nature there was something to behold; we felt blessed to share that space and were amazingly refreshed by the storm. The lake was always sacred to the Aboriginal peoples, and Hayward's home was sacred to him. When that's the case, the feeling is always there for others to share.

You really should visit Gores Landing. There are a number of architectural delights there that were built between 1848 and 1895. It is obvious that, in their incredible and unique styles, these residences were special to their owners.

LONG BEACH

The surveyor Augustus Jones named the beach strip Long Beach in 1791. Anna Jameson, in 1837, described the beach as a very remarkable tongue or slip of land that divided Hamilton Bay from Lake Ontario. This land mass was formed many centuries ago by wind and wave. Marsh plants and bulrushes grew up along the margin of the bay, and, eventually, trees appeared. The Aboriginal peoples followed a trail across the strip, but with the arrival of the white man, who planted orchards and gardens and built a dirt track for a road, the trail was no more.

In the early days, the beach was a naturalist's delight. The silence was broken only by the calls of loons, crows, night hawks, and finches; there were gannets, eagles, and plovers nesting. As many as 134 swans were recorded in one flock. The waters abounded with fish and game birds; whitefish, bass, and pike were plentiful.

At the southern end of Burlington Bay, near the present filtering basins of the Hamilton Waterworks, stood the King's Inn. Governor Simcoe built this large, two-storey, frame house with two wings in 1794. He felt there was a need for a depot for stores and provisions, which would serve as a rendezvous for the military and act as a line of communication with York (Toronto), Detroit, and Niagara. Lady Simcoe described the beach as "a park covered with large spreading oaks." By 1798, several families were also established at the north end of the strip (Wellington Square).

On March 19, 1823, the government was authorized to obtain a loan of five thousand sterling to begin construction of a canal between Burlington Bay and Lake Ontario.

This quaint fishing village ended with the coming of the railway, in 1876. Suddenly crowds from Hamilton and Dundas arrived on hot summer days, on weekends, and on holidays to bask in the sun and cool off in the refreshing waters of Lake Ontario. Establishments such as the Well's Tavern, the Sportsman's Arms, the Cory House, the Dynes Hotel, and the Derry's Hotel were but a few of the many oases of grandeur that awaited, with open doors, to greet visitors and summer residents.

Beach life centred around the entertainment spots. On December 20, 1874, Baldry's Hotel burned to the ground. On the same site, the Ocean House, a three-storey resort, built at a cost of $10,000, was ready to open the following May. This hotel boasted a dance hall, a music salon, a bowling alley, a billiards parlor, and a boat livery. Directly across the road, on the bay side, stood the Royal Yacht Club. The yacht club regattas were often attended by twenty thousand or more people. Band concerts, ball games, and garden parties mostly occurred on the south side of the canal.

Grand summer residences were built by well-to-do Hamiltonians such as Senator W.E. Sanford's wife. Mrs. Sanford built Elisnore, a rest

A Sunday outing at Long Beach, on the bay side of Hamilton.

home for young mothers. The many resorts, with their fancy frames and facades, were social haunts. The owners of homes had earth brought in to replace the sand for landscaped gardens and front lawns. Window boxes were fashionable and nasturtiums grew in the sand.

For many, a romantic evening stroll along the boardwalk to the canal seemed like the thing to do. The automobile era was yet to be. Night time brought the sound of music wafting over water, and the perfume of fruit orchards drifted across the bay on the breeze. No one imagined that such a time would end, but it did.

It started in 1908, when a number of homes on the lakeshore had to be moved to the bay side to allow for a line of towers carrying electric power. The fire of July 17, 1895, had destroyed many of the villas and hotels on the strip, including the Ocean House and the Grand Trunk Pavilion and later the yacht club.

The automobile assisted in this transformation of the beach. The old dirt road gave way to a paved highway in 1923. Summer residences were soon converted to permanent, year-round homes. The wealthy home-owners quickly left the sandy beaches behind. The wonderful amusement park, situated by the canal, continued to operate and generate business at the beach until the late 1970s. The park closed and the bathhouse, the bowling alley, the food-concession booths, the arcade, and a host of rides disappeared forever. The only businesses that remained on Long Beach were one restaurant and two gas stations.

Imagine the joy there would be today if the beach strip had remained.

OAKVILLE

Long before the arrival of European settlers the Mississaugas knew the benefits of locating their camps at the mouths of the rivers that flowed into Lake Ontario between Burlington Bay and Etobicoke Creek.

Besides offering shelter from storms on the lake, the rivers provided the Mississaugas with plenty of fish. On the bottomlands along the west side of Sixteen Mile Creek, where Oakville stands today, the Mississaugas cultivated their cornfields below present-day Riverside Drive. These fields were joined to a summer encampment located on Lake Ontario. A village stood at the foot of present-day Allan Street.

In the wake of the American Revolution, the influx of United Empire Loyalists forced the British Government to negotiate with the Aboriginal peoples to buy land where these people could settle. In the early nineteenth century Upper Canada had few roads, and as a consequence, only the land bordering the waterways was open for settlement.

In 1805, the Mississaugas surrendered their land between Burlington Bay and Etobicoke Creek. Blocks of land at the mouth the Credit River, Sixteen Mile Creek, and Twelve Mile Creek were not purchased by the Crown. These areas were to be used by the Mississaugas as fishing and hunting preserves.

As the population increased, the Mississauga hunting grounds decreased. On February 28, 1820, five chiefs of the Mississaugas surrendered their rights to their reserves at Sixteen Mile Creek and Twelve Mile Creek.

Author's Collection.

Oakville Harbour. It was here on the west side of Sixteen Mile Creek that the Mississaugas cultivated their cornfields near their summer encampment.

William Chisholm began to buy the pine timber in the district that was covered by the Mississauga purchase. He was the son of a Loyalist family and had moved from Nova Scotia to settle on the shores of Burlington Bay in 1794, where he prospered from his business dealings. He owned a fleet of five schooners by the end of 1820.

William Chisholm expressed an interest in the shipping advantages at Sixteen Mile Creek and Lake Ontario. As a result, he arranged with the governor to hold a public auction of the lands on the old Mississauga reserve at the mouth of Sixteen Mile Creek. On July 17, 1827, he bought 960 acres of that land tract for the sum of $4,116.

Chisholm faced three major tasks before he could establish a viable town site at the mouth of Sixteen Mile Creek. First, he had to build a harbour; second, he had to harness Sixteen Mile Creek for enough power to turn the wheels of the grist mill which he planned; and finally he needed to build a storage warehouse.

While the harbour was being established the settlers cleared the land and a village was born. The name of the settlement, suggested by

Chisholm's friend, Robert Baldwin Sullivan, was Oakville, for the white oak trees that flourished there. The timber from these trees was used to manufacture ships.

By the spring of 1830, the harbour had been dredged and a pier of 176 metres constructed. A second pier was well underway by this time. The first hotel was built in the winter of 1827–28 by William Young. It stood at the northeast corner of present-day Colborne and Navy Streets. By 1833, William Wellers' stage line was in operation. A steamship service began the same year with the arrival of the steamer, *Constitution*. The following year, sixteen ships were engaged in exporting wheat, wood, flour, and potash. On the return trip the ships brought back immigrants, as well as supplies.

Today, in the heart of Oakville, south of Lakeshore Road, an area of the old town remains relatively untouched. Original dwellings remain, displaying a period of history never to be experienced again. Ancient oaks continue to thrive, but development has never looked back.

SUDBURY

Sudbury is one of the most important mining centres in the Canadian Shield. Its location on Ramsey Lake and set amidst a range of black, metallic hills with habitually overflowing creeks did not lend itself easily to development. The fact that Sudbury was chosen by the Canadian Pacific Railway as a terminal in 1883 was more by accident than design because at that time Sudbury's future mining potential had yet to be discovered.

In 1871, the original survey of the district was conducted by Sir Sandford Fleming. By 1883, James Worthington had arrived and he named the site after his wife's home in England. A century later, the city of Sudbury, 703 kilometres west of Montreal and 418 kilometres northwest of Toronto, was producing more than one third of the world's nickel. It also became the largest city in Northern Ontario.

Sawmills opened on Lake Ramsey as soon as the area was opened to lumbering, in 1872. Sudbury's town site was surveyed in 1887 by James Morris of Pembroke, and lots were offered for sale by the Canadian Pacific Railway that same year.

One of the first permanent settlers were Dr. and Mrs. William H. Howey, who arrived in 1883. Henry Smith's Sudbury Hotel, a crude log structure, was the first of its kind and stood on the present site of city hall.

Thomas Flanagan, a blacksmith, was the first to notice the copper sulphide in rocks that the railway crews had disturbed in August of 1883. It was not until the following February, however, that application was made to the Ontario government to prospect the land. John Loughrin, who had a contract for cutting railway ties, encouraged Thomas Murray of Pembroke to join him in the venture for the sum of $310. The land was patented in the names of William and Henry Murray, Henry Abbot, and John Loughrin. They called their operation the Murray Mine. It was eventually purchased by Vivian & Sons of Wales, in 1889, and operations began the following year. It was acquired sometime later by the British American Corporation and eventually became part of the International Nickel Company (Inco).

According to Nick and Helma Mika in *Places in Ontario*, "Over the next several years the mining potential of the area was explored, and by 1890, Sudbury was firmly established as a mining centre. In 1886, the Canadian Copper Company, incorporated in Ohio, began operations and the first furnace at Copper Cliff commenced in February of 1889."

During these times, Sudbury was still without sidewalks and sewage ran in open gutters. Drinking water was obtained from a spring that bubbled from a gravel pit.

In 1893, with a population of one thousand citizens, Sudbury was incorporated as a town. That same year, Colonel Robert M. Thompson of New Jersey and Carl Langer of the Mond Chemical Works in England succeeded independently to develop processes for the separation of nickel from nickel-copper ores. Nickel soon eclipsed copper in importance because of the greater potential for products and more market for raw material.

Inco and Mond joined forces in 1929, when they found that progress would be more rapid if they were a single entity. In 1928, Falconbridge Nickel Mines Limited was formed and the first smelter was in operation by 1930.

On August 4, 1930, Sudbury became a city. The population was twenty thousand people.

Today the principal companies operating in the area are Vale, who absorbed Inco, and Xstrata, who absorbed Falconbridge Nickel Mines Limited.

The ebb and flow in the nickel industry is a concern that the labour force in Sudbury cannot ignore. Sudbury's basin once produced 90 percent of the world's nickel. Now it supplies approximately one third and mining as a non-renewable industry will, of necessity, need to be supplanted by something new. What will that be?

SAULT STE. MARIE

Sault Ste. Marie, known as the hub of the Great Lakes, is located between Lake Superior and Lake Huron on the St. Marys River. In 1618, Etienne Brule, an early explorer of the New World, arrived at a location the Ojibwa called the "Meeting Place," a place well established socially, culturally, and economically.

Sault Ste. Marie was incorporated in 1871, and grew in population and industrial reputation until it received city status in 1912. Iron, trees, and water have been the basis for the city's prosperous development, and tourism has grown right along beside it.

The famous Agawa Canyon tour and the summer lock tours in Sault Ste. Marie began attracting attention more than a century ago. Their BonSoo Winter Carnival was conceived by the chamber of commerce as a way of highlighting the great recreational and viable opportunities to be shared in the winter season.

The one-day Agawa Canyon train tour is one of the largest attractions of Sault Ste. Marie. Tourists climb aboard to relax and recline in their seats to gaze out the train window and view the pristine lakes, the incredible gorges, and the valleys of the Algoma Central Country. The 183-kilometre trip leaves Sault Ste. Marie and terminates at Agawa Canyon, where a two-hour stop-over is provided. Photographic opportunities on well-groomed trails abound. Rocky cliffs, waterfalls, and an amazing lookout provide a breathtaking wilderness setting where one can relax, picnic, and even find romance!

Lock Tours Canada operates boat cruises through the famous Soo Locks, one of the busiest canal systems in the world, and alongside giant ships of every kind ply the St. Marys River.

A two-hour sightseeing cruise takes passengers along the shores of both Sault Ste. Marie, Ontario, and Sault Ste. Marie, Michigan, highlighting points of interest. The locks are the last of sixteen water steps in the Great Lakes–St. Lawrence Seaway system, connecting Lake Superior to the Atlantic Ocean more than two thousand miles away. Tourists will pass under the International Bridge, get an extraordinary close-up of the Algoma Steel Corporation, and tour Sault Harbour.

Earnest Hemmingway once remarked in the *Toronto Star Weekly* that the best rainbow trout fishing in the world was in the rapids at the Canadian Soo. To this day the St. Marys River is rated as one of the best trout rivers in the world, and it is part of the waterfront of Sault Ste. Marie. Many species of fish may be found there, including rainbow trout, Atlantic salmon, and three other types of salmon.

During the summer months, native and migratory trout congregate along with Atlantic salmon, which makes for some exciting fishing. Nothing, however, can compare with the population of fall salmon — literally thousands of Chinook and Coho, from August through September and October.

The Sault Ste. Marie museum is an interesting heritage building that was originally built to serve as a post office. Its clock tower is a downtown landmark at the corner of Queen and East Streets. The museum features Superior's Windward Shore, an exhibit tracing the story Algoma District history over the past ten thousand years.

Prehistoric artifacts and frontier farm equipment share the spotlight alongside the story of industrial development. A re-creation of Queen Street invites a stroll past homes as they were in 1912.

To experience Ontario and its history well you really should go north to understand the people, the magnificent landscape, and the sheer power of the scenery along the shores of Lake Superior.

GRAVENHURST AND BRACEBRIDGE

An abundance of lakes and rivers, and a vast expanse of wilderness creates a perpetual, all-season playground. The possibilities are endless. You can sail across a quiet, sun-drenched bay; canoe along an endless shoreline; frolick in refreshing clean waters; or hike on endless trails and stay in standard campgrounds or remote wilderness sites. There are many discoveries to be made in Gravenhurst and Bracebridge.

The town of Gravenhurst is the gateway to the district of Muskoka. The RMS *Segwun* calls Gravenhurst home. This is a fully restored, beautifully appointed ship on Lake Muskoka and Lake Rosseau and from June until Thanksgiving offers dinner cruises, as well as the regular tours that cover a longer season.

On Gravenhurst's smaller lake, Gull Lake, music on the barge is featured each Sunday evening, all summer long. The shoreline offers a gentle sloping grassy area where spectators can listen and enjoy the snippets of entertainment in mellow relaxation.

The main street of Gravenhurst features many unique shops and boutiques. The downtown sports a series of wall murals called "Picture Our Heritage," which are painted on the side walls of buildings and that have recaptured a time when Gravenhurst was a busy timber, railroad, and steamship centre.

The Gravenhurst Opera House is situated on the main street and is home to well-known, professional, live theatre that has been available since 1910.

A family outing in their wooden Viator craft.

The Bethune Memorial House, another popular and restored building, is just around the corner. It is the birthplace of Dr. Norman Bethune and is operated as a museum by Parks Canada. It features the life and times of this famous Canadian doctor who worked in Spain during the Spanish Civil War and who died later in China. The manse home, where he was born in the1890s, is open for the public to tour.

The town in the centre of Muskoka is picturesque Bracebridge. It sits on a hill overlooking a magnificent waterfall on a branch of the Muskoka River. In the summer Bracebridge looks the way Myrtle Beach, South Carolina, looks on March break. The main street is jammed with cars and the sidewalks overflow with pedestrians. Cafes, boutiques, and antique stores line the main street. Several excellent restaurants cater to an influx of visitors who are looking for "dinner experiences."

Many of the shops, offices, and restaurants of Bracebridge have period fronts, celebrating a heritage of grand architecture. At night the town clock, the bell tower, bridge, and the courthouse are illuminated by unique, colourful lighting.

At the top of the falls, by the downtown core is the newly renovated Bird's Mill. This is the last remaining piece of the substantial woollen mill that was built by Henry Bird, and it is now home to the Bracebridge Chamber of Commerce, the Visitor Information Centre, and a delightful restaurant that hangs over the falls.

Bird's impressive home, Woodchester Villa, is set on a hill opposite the same falls. It is a unique, restored historic house. It features a dumb waiter, a fenced widow's walk and has an unusual octagonal shape. Next to it is the Chapel Art Gallery, a showcase for local artists.

The two waterfalls, one on the edge of town, and the readily available power which they provide brought about the development of the town.

Courtesy of the Ontario Archives.

The settlement of Bracebridge, circa 1880.

Bracebridge was the first municipality in the province to own its own hydro-electric station, in 1894. The present power plant at the foot of the falls is the oldest power plant in Canada that is in continuous use. Follow the illustrated markers around Bracebridge for other glimpses of the town's rich history.

Bracebridge Bay Park is at the base of the falls, with tennis courts and a playground. It is an ideal setting for picnicking and swimming. Just downriver is the dock of the Lake Muskoka, a one-hundred-passenger cruise ship that tours the river and Lake Muskoka daily, all summer long.

The most famous attraction in Bracebridge is Santa's Village. Old Saint Nick has been summering in Bracebridge for forty years now, and he has a great playground for kids of all ages. Ride the ferris wheel, the roller coaster, or paddle boat. For teens, Rudolph's Funland has go-karts, batting cages, mini-golf, or roller blading. There is even an incredible state-of-the-art activity centre.

Take a drive this summer to Gravenhurst and Bracebridge some-time, and enjoy everything this geographical area has to offer — even Christmas in the summer!

The Bala summer train station located near the Bala Bay Hotel.

COCHRANE

The Cochrane district in the northern part of Ontario covers an area of more than 35.5 million acres of land, with a population of more than 87,000. It is bound to the north by James Bay and the Albany River, to the east by Quebec, to the south by the Districts of Timiskaming, Sudbury, and Algoma, and to the west by Thunder Bay.

The area was once known only to roving bands of Aboriginal peoples until the fur traders created trails that connected the scattered Hudson's Bay Company posts.

Although the first settlement in the district was one of these fur trading posts, located at Moose Factory in 1673, it was not until the discovery of gold at the beginning of the twentieth century, at Night Hawk, that the southern part of the district was opened up for settlement.

As early as 1884, a group of businessmen began to discuss the possibility of building a railway from North Bay to James Bay. The first step toward construction was made in 1900, connecting North Bay with New Liskeard. The line was known as the Temiskaming and Northern Ontario Railway. The railway was completed to Moosonee on July 15, 1932. The name of the railway was changed in 1945 to the Ontario Northland Railway.

The town of Cochrane, located on Highway 11, at the junction of the Canadian National Railway and the Ontario Northland Railway, was named in honour of Frank Cochrane, Ontario Minister of Lands and Forests in the early 1900s.

The town site chosen by engineer Joseph E. Burke as the terminal point for the Northern Ontario Railway had long been known to fur traders who frequently camped at Norman Lake, now part of Drury Park, on their way north to Moose Factory.

The site was laid out in 1908, and in November of that year a public sale of lots was held. The railway's plan for the town specified lots to buy 66 by 120 feet on seventeen avenues one hundred feet wide and running north and south, with seven smaller streets running east and west. This plan never materialized. Most of the lots were never cleared properly, and those which were not sold at the auction were never cleared at all.

Cochrane has been known for heavy snowfalls in the past and present times.

The first homes were built so close together that fire was a very real threat in the early days. Cochrane's core was destroyed by fire in 1910, a few months after the settlement had been incorporated as a town. It was rebuilt, but badly burned again in the porcupine fire of 1911, and once more in 1916, when the town was almost totally destroyed.

In 1911, the town had a population of three thousand settlers. Water, electricity, and telephone services were being installed at that time.

By the 1920s, Cochrane had evolved from a frontier settlement to a prosperous community. Although primarily a railroad town, lumber and farming played a major role in its economy and employed as many people as the railway did.

The discovery of mineral wealth in the area accelerated the growth of the town and it quickly became an important supply and shipping centre for the area. Cochrane's economy was further enhanced by tourism. The popular Polar Bear Express, conveying visitors by rail on one-day excursions in the summer from Cochrane to Moosonee on James Bay, became a major tourist attraction.

Housed in old railway cars, Cochrane's railway and pioneer museum is located east of the railway station and recalls the early days of settlement in the Cochrane area.

Cochrane today offers all the conveniences and services of a well-planned community, arisen like the phoenix from the ashes of earlier fires.

RODMAN HALL, ST. CATHARINES

The strength and dignity of Rodman Hall reflects the character of the man who owned it, Thomas Rodman Merritt.

Thomas Merritt, born in St. Catharines on October 17, 1824, was the fourth son of the Honourable William Hamilton Merritt, the man responsible for the building of the Welland Canal. Thomas spent his early years amid the busy scenes of his father's mercantile and political life. He began his own business career in 1843, operating a large general store with a partner, James Rea Benson. He later branched out by purchasing a flour mill, and in connection with his mill, he ran an extensive fleet of vessels to carry his produce to the seaboard.

Over the years Merritt pursued other business interests in the Niagara region. With his father and others he had reorganized the Niagara District Bank in 1854 at St. Catharines, and he served as vice-president until its merger in 1875, into the Imperial Bank of Canada, of which he also became vice-president and, in 1902, president. He was a director and president of the Niagara Falls Suspension Bridge Company and president of the Security Loan and Savings Company.

Merritt undertook responsibilities in the political sphere, serving as a town councillor and later a member of senate. As a devout Anglican, he took part in the founding of the Bishop Ridley College, a boys' school, set up at St. Catharines, in 1888.

In 1853, he began construction of Rodman Hall. The charm of the house on the hill was in the park-like setting and the landscaped grounds.

Virtually barren land when construction began, it was soon planted with exotic trees and flowering shrubs that enhanced the stylish home. Enchanting walkways bordered sweeping lawns, partially shaded by pine, maple, willow, and black walnut trees. To the east of the house, hidden among birch trees, once stood a summerhouse where the ladies took tea.

When Rodman Hall was completed, Thomas moved in with his new bride, Mary Benson. The couple lived to celebrate their fiftieth wedding anniversary there in 1903.

Rodman Hall remained in the Merritt family until 1959 when T.R. Merritt, Esq., sold it to the St. Catharines Art Association. The council renovated it into an arts centre, with a new gallery built onto the drawing room. In 1974, the National Museums of Canada announced that it had selected Rodman Hall as a national exhibition centre.

Between the foyer and the main hall is a stained-glass partition bearing the Merritt coat of arms. To the left of the hall two drawing rooms were once adorned with Bohemian crystal chandeliers imported from Paris. Now this area is used for art rental and exhibition space. The room used as a gift shop, on the right, was originally an oak-panelled dining room. Through the swinging door was the butler's pantry, now the kitchen. The long hallway leading to the right off the main hall passes the former library, and is now a tea room. Halfway up the main staircase is an imported stained-glass window, and the room to the right of the stairs on the second floor, now the boardroom, was the upstairs living or morning room. The other rooms on this level were all bedrooms, with the exception of one at the top of the back staircase (now the education office), which was then a billiards room. The third floor had four bedrooms and two storage rooms.

Rodman Hall has a permanent collection of approximately 850 works of art by nineteenth and twentieth century Canadian, American, and European artists. It presents a year-round exhibition program featuring contemporary, historical, regional, national, and international works of art, as well as functioning as a performance venue for Niagara musicians.

Since Rodman Hall Arts Centre was first established, more than three hundred exhibitions, such as works of James Morrice, David Milne, and Emily Carr have been presented. The strength and dignity carry on.

BIBLIOGRAPHY

BOOKS

Aykroyd, Peter H., with Angela Narth. *A History of Ghosts*. New York: Rodale Books, 2009.

Barrett, Henry B. *Lore and Legends of Long Point*. Aylmer, Ontario: Aylmer Express, 2000.

Boyle, Terry. *Haunted Mississauga*. Rosseau, Ontario: Entwood Cottage Editions, 2006.

———. *Hidden Ontario: Secrets from Ontario's Past*, second edition. Toronto: Dundurn, 2011.

———. *Ontario Memories*. Toronto: Polar Bear Press, 1998.

———. *Under This Roof: Family Homes of Southern Ontario*. Toronto: Doubleday Canada, 1980.

Colombo, John Robert. *True Canadian UFO Stories*. Toronto: Key Porter Books, 2004.

Conway, Thor. *Spirits on Stone: The Agawa Pictographs*. Echo Bay, Ontario: Heritage Discoveries, 1990.

Corso, Colonel Philip J., with William J. Barnes. *The Day After Roswell: A Former Pentagon Official Reveals the U.S. Government's Shocking UFO Cover-Up*. New York: Pocket Books, 1997.

Davis, Carole and Brian Hadley-James. *The Skull Speaks*. Toronto: Amhrea Publishing, 1985.

Foote, David K., with Daniel Stoffman. *Boom, Bust and Echo: Profiting from the Demographic Shift in the 21st Century*. Toronto: Stoddart Publishing Co., 2001.

Guiley, Rosemary Ellen. *The Encyclopedia of Ghosts and Spirits*. New York: Checkmark Books, 2007.

Hamilton, James Cleland. *The Georgian Bay: An Account of its Position, Inhabitants, Mineral Interests, Fish, Timber and Other Resources*. Toronto: James Bain & Son, 1893.

Hamilton, T. Glen. *Intention and Survival: Physical Research Studies and the Bearing of Intentional Actions by Trance Personalities on the Problem of Human Survival*. Toronto: Macmillan, 1942.

Helliwell, Tanis. *Summer with the Leprechauns*. Powell River, British Columbia: Tanis Helliwell Corporation, 2011.

Joseph, Frank. *Discovering the Mysteries of Ancient America: Lost History and Legends, Unearthed and Explored*. Franklin Lakes, New Jersey: New Page Books, 2006.

Killan, Gerald. *David Boyle: From Artisan to Archaeologist*. Toronto: University of Toronto Press, 1983.

Korff, Kal K. *The Roswell UFO Crash: What They Don't Want You to Know*. New York: Prometheus Books, 1997.

MacKay, Donald. *Flight From Famine: The Coming of the Irish to Canada*. Toronto: McClelland & Stewart, 1991.

Martin, Norma, Catherine Milne, and Donna McGillis. *Gore's Landing and The Rice Lake Plains*. Gores Landing, Ontario: Heritage Gores Landing, 1986.

Mika, Nick. *Places in Ontario: Their Name Origins and History*. Belleville, Ontario: Mika Publishing Company, 1977.

O'Meara, Michael. *Oil Springs: The Birthplace of the Oil Industry in North America, 1858–1958*. Centennial Historical Committee, 1958.

Penwyche, Gossamer. *The World of Fairies*. New York: Sterling Publishing, 2001.

Robertson, J. Ross, and Elizabeth Simcoe. *The Diary of Mrs. John Graves Simcoe, Wife of the First Lieutenant-Governor of the Province of Upper Canada, 1792–96*. Toronto: William Briggs, 1911.

Robinson, James F. *Amazing Tales from Eastern Ontario*. Belleville, Ontario: Mika Publishing Company, 1987.

Suzuki, David, and Peter Knudtson. *Wisdom of the Elders: Native and Scientific Ways of Knowing About Nature.* Vancouver: Greystone Books, 1993.

NEWSPAPERS

Lamb, Jamie. "Muskoka Man Faces Spacecraft Creature." *The Packet News.* Bracebridge, Ontario, October 1975.

INDEX

Numbers in italics indicate images.

Algonquin Park, 114

Asia (steamer), 55, *56*, 58

Bancroft, 12, 50–51, 69

Bayly, Governor Charles, 202

Beatty Lines, 59

Bennett, Prime Minister R.B., 37–38

Bigelow, Joseph, 128–30

Bowmanville, 95

Boyle, David, 113–14, 136–38, 199

Bracebridge, 108, 219–22

Brockville, 175, 176

Brooklin, 12, 179–80

Brougham Apple Basket, 48–49

Bruce Trail, 98

Burkett, Captain, 60–61

Burlington, 30, 45

Burlington Bay, 209, 210, 212–13

Burwell, Malcolm, 159

Canadian Shield, 68, 215

Casa Loma, 167–68

Cobden, 69

Cobourg, 11–13, 22, 27–28, 169–71, 208

Cochrane, 204–05, 223–225

Coldwater, 96

Collingwood, 12, 17, 59–62, 154–56

Conant, Roger, 200–01

Cornwall, 12, 177–78

Darlington, 200

Elora, 137, 197–99

First Nations
    Chippewa, 96, 157
    Cree, 202–05
    Huron, 96
    Iroquois, 97, 162, 181
    Mississauga, 114, 181, 212–13
    Ojibwa, 77–78, 96–97, 146, 162, 206, *207*, 217

First World War, 34, 102, 136
Fleetwood Creek Natural Area, 43
Foote, David K., 52–53
Fort Charles, 203
Fort Michilimackinac, 191
Franklin, Sir John, 133–35, 163
Fraser Lake, 12, 69
French River, 55, 82–84
Frontenac Axis, 68

Galt, 72, 189, 197
Galt, John, 197
Gananoque River, 69
Georgian Bay, 17–19, 55, 58, 59,
    138, 154
Gores Landing, 142, 168, 206–08
Gravenhurst, 219–22
Great Depression, 36–39, 145
Grey Owl, 144–46
Guelph, 197

Hamilton, 32, 45, 138, 149, 210
Hamilton, Dr., 102–04
Hayward, Gerald Sinclair, 141–43,
    168, 208
Hudson Bay, 202–04
Hudson's Bay Company, 163,
    202–04, 223
Huntsville, 73

Ivanhoe, 135

Kawartha Region Conservation
    Authority, 43
Ken Reid Conservation Area, 42

Kincardine, 12, 132, 194–96
Kingston, 22, 23, 25, 68, 125, 126,
    163, 165, 167, 184
Kinsale, 48
Kirkfield, 168, 172–74

Lake Couchiching, 95–96
Lake Erie, 65, 66, 111, 159, 186, 189
Lake Huron, 18, 59, 154, 162, 163,
    191, 194, 195, 203, 217
Lake Ontario, 12, 25, 68, 154, 169,
    170, 171, 186, 200, 207, 209,
    210, 212, 213
Lake Simcoe, 96
Lake Superior, 53, 77, 203, 217, 218
Lindsay, 42, 43, 128
Little Current, 55
London, 45, 159–61
Long Point, 12, 65–67
Loyalists. See United Empire
    Loyalists

Macdonald, Prime Minister Sir
    John A., 127, 141
Mackenzie, Sir William, 172–74
Mackenzie King, Prime Minister
    William Lyon, 103
MacTaggert, John, 23, 25
McLaughlin, Sam, 38
Merritt, Thomas, 226–27
Midland, 155
Ministry of Natural Resources and
    Forestry, 114
Moose Factory, 202–05

Niagara Falls, 186–88
Niagara Peninsula, 32
Niagara-on-the-Lake, 188, 200
North West Company, 197

Oak Ridges Moraine, 43
Oakville, 45, 212–14
Oil Springs, 149–53
Ontario Heritage Foundation, 43
Orillia, 79, 95–97
Oshawa, *38*, 129, 180, 200–01
Ottawa Valley, 22, 162
Owen Sound, 17, 55, *56*

Paris, 189–90
Parry Sound, *46*, *57*, 58, 59–61,
    83, 155
Pellatt, Sir Henry Mill, 167–68
Penetanguishene, 155, 162
Perri, Rocco, 32
Perth, 22, 175–76
Peterborough, 22, 26, 40, 113, 138,
    207
Petrolia, 151–52
Pigeon River Headwaters
    Conservation Area, 43
Port Hope, 141, 165–66, 207
Port Perry, 105–07, 128–30, 179,
    181
Port Stanley, 65
Prohibition, 32–35
Project Magnet, 12, 89, 91–94
Project Second Story, 92
Project Theta, 92. *See also* Project
    Second Story

Rama, 96
Ramsey, David, 12, 65
Rebellion of 1837. *See* Upper
    Canada Rebellion
Red Horse Lake, 69
Reid, George, 131–32
Reynolds, Sheriff Nelson, 125–27,
    168
Rice Lake, 112, 113, *137*, 141–43,
    168, 206–08
Rideau Canal, 23, 25, 176
Rideau Lake, 25
Robinson, Peter, 22, 24

Sarnia, 12, 149, 157–58
Sault Ste. Marie, 55, *56*, 77, 162,
    217–18
Scugog Island, 12, 107, 181–82
Second World War, 35, 39, 71,
    171, 192
Shingleton Lake, 69
Shirley's Bay, 92–93
Southampton, 12, 162–64, 196
Spratley, Ken, 48–49
St. Catharines, 12, 45, 55, 68, 73,
    226–27
St. Thomas, 80, 205
Starvation Bay, 82, *84*
Stirling, 183–85
Stoffman, Daniel, 52
Sudbury, 215–16

T. Eaton Company, 38
Talbot, Colonel Thomas, 159
Toronto, 30, 36, *39*, 129, 131, 132,

134, 137, 138, 154, 178, 192,
199, 209, 215
Trent University, 40
Troyer, John, 12, 66–67

United Empire Loyalists, 36, 45,
177, 187, 212, 213
University of Toronto, 51, 52
Upper Canada Rebellion, 125, 201

Victoria County, 42–44

War of 1812, 46, 175, 191, 200
Wasaga Beach, 191–93
Waubuno, 59–62
Wellington County, 136, 138
Whitby, 12, 120–22, 126, 127, 128,
129, 168, 179, 180
Whitefish, 73
Williams, Commander John
Tucker, 165–66
Williams, James, 149–50
Windsor, 33
Wingham, 131–32
World War I. *See* First World War
World War II. *See* Second World
War

Yellowhead, Chief, 96

BY THE SAME AUTHOR

Haunted Ontario 4
Terry Boyle

Meet the forever-beautiful spectre of Marilyn Monroe, who came to the French River seeking sanctuary from fame and fans, and decided to stay. Journey to the remarkable Victorian Beild House Inn in Collingwood; sleep in the bed of King Edward VIII of England, and wait for the deceased doctor to make a room call. Acquaint yourself with the lonely woman who searches empty rooms and narrow hallways of the Grafton Village Inn. She glides up the central staircase to the ballroom, where she fades from sight. Who is the mysterious woman dressed in white-satin at the Joseph Brant Museum? Is she searching for a door that will lead to freedom? Musket in hand, a sentry paces the grounds of Fort George, prepared for the next American invasion. Does he know he is a casualty of time, not war?

With a list of addresses, phone numbers, and websites for each location, Terry Boyle invites all ghost enthusiasts along for some adventure. Feeling brave? This could be the perfect itinerary for your next trip.

Haunted Ontario 3
Terry Boyle

Interested in discovering more about haunted Ontario? Join Terry Boyle as he explores the shadowlands beyond the grave. Revel in the outstanding evidence of spirit habitation in museums, historic homes, inns, jails, and graveyards. Witness the full apparition of the innkeeper's wife at Greystones Inn in Orangeville. Encounter the misty form of a civil war veteran in the graveyard of the old St. Thomas church. Experience the incredible slamming-of-doors at the Keefer Mansion in Thorold. Visit a whole village of spirits who share the buildings at Black Creek Pioneer Village. You can even spend the entire night in the Orillia Opera House with Terry and his friends.

Prepare to be scared out of your wits with the stories behind these and other hauntings. After providing you with a list of addresses, phone numbers, and websites for each location, Terry invites you and all other ghost enthusiasts along for the adventure. Feeling brave?

Hidden Ontario
Terry Boyle

Terry Boyle unveils the eccentric and bizarre in these mini-histories of Ontario's towns and cities: the imposter who ran the Rockwood Asylum in Kingston; Ian Fleming's inspiration for James Bond; the Prince of Wales's undignified crossing of Rice Lake; the tragic life of Joseph Brant; the man who advertised his wife's death before poisoning her; as well as Ontario's first bullfight and the answer to the question, "Why did so many lumberjacks sport beards?"

The colourful characters, Native legends, and incredible tales that make up our province's fascinating past come alive in *Hidden Ontario*. From Bancroft, Baldoon, and Brighton to Timmins, Toronto, and Trenton, find out more about the Ontario you thought you knew.

CPSIA information can be obtained at www.ICGtesting.com
Printed in the USA
LVOW07s0954100916

504050LV00020B/322/P